Cuban women:
Changing roles and
population trends

* Centre for Demographic Studies, University of Havana.
⁺ Federation of Cuban Women.

Women, Work and Development, 17

Cuban women: Changing roles and population trends

S. Catasús,* A. Farnós,* F. González,*
R. Grove,+ R. Hernández* and B. Morejón*

Prepared with the financial support of the
United Nations Fund for Population Activities
(UNFPA)

International Labour Office   Geneva

ISBN 92-2-106387-9
ISSN 0253-2042

First published 1988

Printed by the International Labour Office, Geneva, Switzerland

PREFACE

The study described in this monograph was conducted in the context of an ILO global research project entitled "Demographic Change and the Roles of Women", which was funded by the United Nations Fund for Population Activities (UNFPA).

The work conducted in Cuba was divided into two stages. The first consisted of a historical review of existing documentation and statistics concerning fertility and the situation of women in Cuba. The results of this review can be found in a chapter by Alfonso Farnós, Fernando González and Raúl Hernández in the ILO publication <u>Working women in socialist countries: The fertility connection</u> (1985), edited by Richard Anker and Valentina Bodrova.

The second part of the study involved conducting a survey of Cuban women in three very diverse areas of Cuba in order to obtain the more detailed information required to improve our understanding of how the changing situation of women is related to demographic changes, in particular declining infant mortality and fertility. The results of this investigation form the basis for the present monograph.

The survey was carried out by a group of specialists from the Demographic Studies Centre of the University of Havana and from the Cuban Women's Federation under the direction of Fernando González. Fifth year students in economics and psychology at the University of Havana took part as interviewers and members of the Federation of Cuban Women also participated in the field-work stage of the investigation.

The analysis of the results and the writing of the present monograph was done by Sonia Catasús, Alfonso Farnós, Fernando González, Rosario Grove, Raúl Hernandez and Blanca Morejón. Special mention should be made of the hard work done by Raúl Hernández who was responsible for the unification of style and the final presentation of the text both in English and in the original Spanish version. We should also like to acknowledge the work done by the ILO in reorganising the text to produce a more condensed version for English-speaking readers.

It would not have been possible to carry out this study without the useful co-operation given by the Grass-roots Organisation of the Cuban Women's Federation and by the women interviewed.

v

CONTENTS

FIGURES

TABLES

CHAPTER I

INTRODUCTION

Major economic, social and political events have taken place in Cuba since the Revolution in 1959. Conspicuous in this respect are two interrelated aspects of socio-economic development that are the focus of this monograph: women's increased status and participation in the economy and in society; and a transition to low mortality and low fertility rates. By the beginning of the 1980s, Cuba had passed through the last phase of the demographic transition, since both fertility rates and mortality rates were at levels observed in developed countries with fertility well below replacement levels and life expectancy at birth above 70 years. At the same time, owing to rapid increases in women's economic participation, women constituted well over one-third of the formal sector labour force by the 1980s.

From the first decades of the present century, Cuban fertility has been considered as moderate for a developing country. The changes brought about by the Revolution in 1959 resulted, at first, in an increase in fertility, but this only lasted until around 1965. Subsequently the decrease in Cuban fertility has been one of the most dramatic in human history. Between 1971 and 1981 the crude birth rate of the country dropped from 29.5 to 14.0 births per thousand inhabitants, and the gross reproduction rate over the same period decreased from 1.92 to 0.78 daughters per woman (CEE, 1984, pp. 47 and 51). Thus, fertility rates in the early 1980s have become lower than in many developed countries and considerably below replacement levels if sustained over the long run.

The reasons for the rapid fertility decline in Cuba have been the subject of considerable international interest and debate because of their potential implications for policies in developing countries which are seeking ways to reduce fertility levels (see ILO, 1984, for example). Many would be interested in learning how and why a developing country such as Cuba has been able to obtain such low fertility rates without any coercion or specific population policy. The answer is, of course, complex since many changes have occurred simultaneously in Cuba and no one factor is likely to have been responsible for this fertility decline.

Some of the main transformations since 1959 are reviewed here to provide the context for understanding how the changing roles of women may be related to the rapid decline of fertility in Cuba.

Agrarian reform was a priority of the Revolution. Share-croppers, tenant farmers and other poor agricultural workers were given full title to land, and most latifundia (large estates and plantations belonging to one person or enterprise) were expropriated and transformed into state farms. The creation of large agricultural and livestock enterprises allowed the gradual application of advanced techniques to agricultural production. By 1981, about 76 per cent of the agricultural workforce was employed on state farms (CEE, 1983). In rural areas, agricultural employment of women has risen, in particular for fruit and vegetable cultivation and for work in battery farms for egg production.

The ideal that all members of society should have equal possibilities of participating in that society made education a first-order objective of the Revolution. A massive extension of education was considered fundamental to the construction of a new society in Cuba. Education was made free at all levels and large investments were made in new buildings, especially in rural areas. At the primary level (up to the sixth grade), enrolment of both sexes is now almost 100 per cent. At the other levels, enrolment has been continuously increasing. As an indication of the educational advances being made by women, it can be noted that the proportion of women among registered university students has increased steadily in recent years - reaching 36 per cent in 1974 and 48 per cent in 1980 (CEE, unpublished information).

The provision of free health services and their extension to all areas of the country was another priority of the Revolution. In 1959, there was only one rural hospital and a few polyclinics in all of Cuba. By 1970, there were 53 rural hospitals and 378 polyclinics. During the 1970s, there were 213 inhabitants per hospital bed compared with 91 in the USSR, 171 in the United States (1980) and 812 in Mexico (WHO, 1983). Infant mortality declined from 79 deaths per thousand births in 1953 to 19 in 1980 (Farnos, Gonzalez and Hernandez, 1985, p. 200). This decline in infant mortality is linked not only to the extension of health services but also to the improved educational levels of women since, as in many countries, surveys in Cuba have found an inverse relationship between the mother's educational level and infant mortality (CEE, 1982). Current levels of infant mortality are thus very low for a developing country and approaching those of developed countries: for example, in industrialised market economy countries, infant mortality averaged about 10 per thousand in the 1980s (World Bank, 1984, table 230).

A particularly important aspect of change in Cuba is the

rapid improvement in the situation of women and increasing sexual equality in culture, society, employment and the economy, owing to the Government's ideological commitment to equality of the sexes and policy measures which were taken to improve the position of women. The new conditions and conceptions of the Cuban State, together with the new legislation relating to women, assure them the right to work, guarantee them the same salary as men for equal work, paid vacations, free access to all the professions, and the right to draw social security, while yet other laws aim to give them the maximum protection in their dual role as mothers and workers.

Important changes have occurred in the participation of women in the labour force[1] as well as in their distribution across occupations. It is estimated that in 1953, women comprised 13 per cent of the economically active population (CEDEM, 1976) compared with about one-third in 1981. In the earlier period, the majority of economically active women were in domestic service (estimated at 70 per cent in 1958) whereas in 1980, women constituted approximately 53 per cent of professionals and technicians and 82 per cent of administrative workers (Federation of Cuban Women, no date). These employment changes have occurred not only because of increasing employment opportunities for women but also because of improvements in female educational levels.

Political and mass organisations also help to incorporate women - workers, students and housewives - into the economic and social life of the country. Also, through these organisations women are involved in voluntary tasks which benefit the community, such as infant vaccination and other campaigns developed by the health and hygiene brigades, or working with young people with behaviour problems. The Federation of Cuban Women, which co-ordinates and promotes these tasks, also encourages the Movement of Militant Mothers for Education, which is responsible for ensuring that schools maintain adequate standards and for drawing up recreational and vacation plans, in conjunction with the schools themselves. This movement, which is growing all the time, now has 1.6 million women members which represents 51.7 per cent of the female population of 17 years old and over. In the different organisations in which women take part, there are study meetings about female problems, the role of the family, the education of children, child care, the new moral conceptions, norms of social behaviour, and topics of general interest, which help to broaden their knowledge and outlook.

Major changes have also occurred with respect to marriage and divorce. In the Family Code of 1976, marriage no longer has the economic character of a civil contract as conveyed in the old Social Defence Code but is redefined as the voluntary and equal partnership of a man and a woman. Marriage rates per thousand population increased rapidly in the late 1960s reaching a peak of 11.3 per thousand in 1971 (Farnos, Gonzalez and Hernandez, 1985). At the same time divorce rates increased from 0.4 per thousand population in 1959 to 1.8 in 1968 and 3.2 in 1971 - one of the highest rates in the world.

The situation of Cuban women has thus undergone a profound change within the framework of the transformations which have taken place in the past 25 years. These transformations, acting primarily on the economic structure, have in turn affected elements of the ideological superstructure such as the culture and individual and socio-political activity and values relating to the family and children. Women, as an important part of Cuban society, have been actively involved in the process of transformation.

The purpose of this monograph is to document the economic, cultural and social changes which have in fact taken place for Cuban women, both at the family and at the societal levels, and to analyse the effects these changes have had on demographic behaviour during the last two decades, in particular in relation to fertility and infant mortality.

When studying the changing situation of women, we will concentrate on the following three factors: the incorporation of women into the formal labour force, in directly productive sectors as well as in services; the improvement in women's educational and cultural levels; and women's participation in the political and social life of the country.

In this monograph, the study of these factors is linked to changes in women's roles in the family, the division of work within the family, child-care practices (in particular relating to children under one year old) and the combination of women's work in the family and their economic activity. In this way the changing roles of women in Cuban society are related to the demographic changes which have taken place since 1959.

The general hypothesis presented in this study is that Cuban women, since the Revolution of 1959, have found favourable conditions to increase their participation in the economic, political and social life of the country. This has enabled the roles of women both in society and in the family to be transformed, and this trend has in turn helped to bring about major demographic changes in Cuban society.

The particular hypotheses investigated in this monograph are the following:
(a) women's increased participation in the labour force has brought about changes in reproductive behaviour, including low levels of fertility;
(b) women's improved educational and cultural levels have also

played a part in lowering fertility;

(c) although a significant proportion of women are still not incorporated directly in the formal labour force, the changing economic and social context of the country has resulted in a pattern of reproductive behaviour on the part of such women similar to that shown by those who are economically active;

(d) although the country already has very low fertility levels, there are still some large differences between the urban and rural zones which can be explained by socio-economic differences.

The idea of this research was to test these hypotheses and to throw further light on the roles of women in present-day Cuban society. For this purpose, a survey of 3,302 women was undertaken on the roles of women and demographic change (EDEMU-82). In order to obtain as representative a sample as possible, the sample was restricted to women aged 15 to 59 years, and three different socio-economic areas of the country were chosen: an urban area, the Municipality of Plaza de la Revolución, in the province of City of Havana, capital of Cuba; a rural mountainous area, the Municipality of Yateras, in the Guantánamo province; and in order to obtain intermediate levels with respect both to fertility and to degree of urbanisation, the district of Buenavista, a suburban area located in the Municipality of Cienfuegos, in the province of the same name, in the centre of the country. In all, 1,589 women were interviewed in Plaza, 817 in Buenavista, and 896 in Yateras. The method of sampling used was that of single stage cluster sampling with probability proportional to size (see Appendix 1).

The results obtained with this sample are not, obviously, valid for all provinces, nor for the country as a whole, considering the size of the sample. However, choosing areas with a broad range of characteristics has enabled us to draw some conclusions, taking into account the nature of the changes which have occurred in each area and the differences which still exist in the country.

This monograph consists of eight chapters. In Chapter II we present the geographic, socio-economic and demographic characteristics of the areas studied. The purpose of this chapter is to provide a frame of reference in relation to the characteristics already mentioned.

Chapter III characterises the situation of women in accordance with the information obtained by the survey in each of the three study areas, looking particularly at the changes experienced by women between generations and in different areas. The educational and cultural levels attained by women, women's participation in economic activity and women in the context of the family are the main topics dealt with in this chapter.

Chapter IV presents a study of fertility. It analyses some estimates of fertility obtained in the survey and looks at its different characteristics according to area and age group.

Chapter V looks at women's ideals relating to family size and the spacing of births, and compares these ideals with actual reproductive behaviour. It also examines the relationship between reproductive behaviour and socio-economic factors such as educational level, standard of living and women's participation in economic activity, and the relationship between this behaviour and fertility levels.

Chapter VI takes as its subject nuptiality patterns in Cuba, as these obviously have a very direct relationship with fertility. Ideal and actual age at first marriage, marital status, and marital stability are all covered, as well as the relationships between these and the socio-economic factors already discussed in preceding chapters.

Chapter VII looks at the use of abortion and contraception to control fertility, and the relationship between such use and fertility levels, contrasting particularly the trends found in the urban area of Plaza de la Revolución and in the rural area of Yateras. The relationship between the incidence of abortion and level of contraceptive use and key socio-economic factors is also discussed.

The general results of the work are summarised in Chapter VIII.

Note

[1] The authors are aware that considerable problems are inherent in the labour force concepts and the meaning of "economic activity", particularly with respect to the subsistence type of activities in which women engage (see, for example, Anker, 1983). However, in order to be able to analyse trends and utilise comparative data from earlier surveys and censuses, the conventional definition (as detailed in Appendix 5) is used throughout. These data are, in all probability, reasonably accurate with respect to formalised and monetised types of employment.

CHAPTER II

THE AREAS OF STUDY: GEOGRAPHIC, ECONOMIC AND
DEMOGRAPHIC CHARACTERISTICS

In order to contribute to a better understanding and
interpretation of the results of the survey, the main
geographic, economic and demographic characteristics which
differentiate the three areas studied are discussed here.
Direct observation of the situation at a provincial level also
offers a general framework of reference for the analysis as a
whole which can sometimes remedy the lack of official
statistical information in each of the areas.

2.1 Geographic characteristics

The female population studied is settled in the
municipalities of Plaza de la Revolución and Yateras and the
district of Buenavista in the municipality of Cienfuegos, in the
provinces of City of Havana, Guantánamo and Cienfuegos,
respectively.

Figure 1 shows the geographic location of these three areas
which are in the western, eastern and central regions of the
country respectively.

Plaza de la Revolución, a very populous and completely
urbanised municipality, with a density of over 13,000
inhabitants per square kilometre, presents a great contrast with
Yateras, a mountainous region with an altitude of 300-900 metres
above sea level, watered by the hydrographic system of Cuba's
largest river, the Toa. Yateras is one of the only two
municipalities of the country with a completely rural
population, with an average density of less than 30 inhabitants
per square kilometre. The municipality of Cienfuegos, where the
suburban district of Buenavista is located, has as its most
important geographic feature Cienfuegos Bay, which is large and
has excellent port conditions, surrounded by waterways which
irrigate well-developed agricultural zones. It is on one of
these waterways, that of the Caonao river, that the Buenavista
district is located, only 3 kilometres from the centre of
Cienfuegos, a city of more than 100,000 inhabitants and capital
city of the province of the same name.

8

Figure 1: Location of survey areas

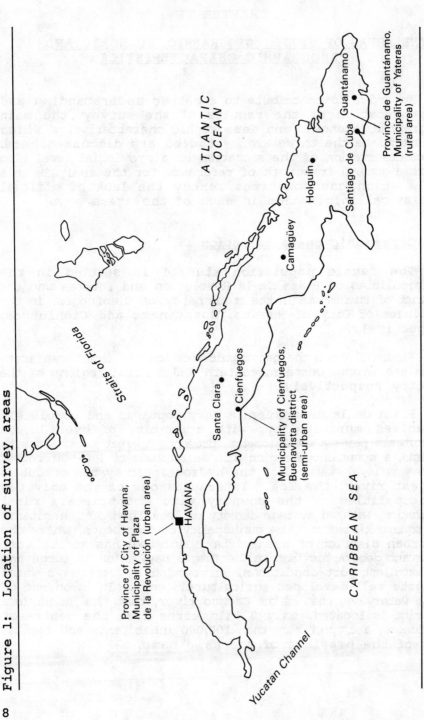

Straits of Florida

ATLANTIC OCEAN

0°0′

Province of City of Havana,
Municipality of Plaza
de la Revolución (urban area)

HAVANA

Santa Clara

Cienfuegos

Municipality of Cienfuegos,
Buenavista district
(semi-urban area)

CARIBBEAN SEA

Camagüey

Holguín

Santiago de Cuba

Guantánamo

Province de Guantánamo,
Municipality of Yateras
(rural area)

Yucatan Channel

2.2 Economic characteristics

Each of the municipalities studied is economically specialised, but in different ways. The predominant economic activities in Plaza de la Revolución involve services and public administration, the municipality being the seat of government and the main educational and cultural centre of the country. Yateras, on the other hand, has important forest reserves while coffee growing is the main economic activity. In the municipality of Cienfuegos, economic activity is basically directed towards the industrial, chemical and electrical power industries, though agriculture and the ports absorb some of the labour force.

This clear economic differentiation of the areas studied in its turn affects the level of female participation in economic activity.

Table 1. <u>Activity rate by sex of the population aged 15 years and over in the areas of study, 1981</u> (percentages)

Area of study	Male	Female
Plaza de la Revolución	71.7	49.3
Cienfuegos	71.9	38.8
Yateras	67.3	28.7
Province		
City of Havana	72.1	43.2
Cienfuegos	72.4	38.6
Guantánamo	67.4	27.4

Source: Comité Estatal de Estatísticas (CEE), (1983), Vols. II, III and VIII, figures 5.3 and 3, pp. CIV, CVI and CII respectively.

Table 1 gives the activity rates by sex of the population aged 15 years and over. The highest values for female participation are shown in the province of City of Havana and its municipality Plaza de la Revolución, where employment is very concentrated in the non-productive sphere; Guantánamo and Yateras have the lowest levels of female economic activity, while Cienfuegos occupies an intermediate position. This can be explained by the industrial development which has taken place during recent years, bringing greater diversification of employment to the region.

These findings are confirmed when the structure of the economically active population is analysed by sphere and sector of the economy for each of the areas studied (see table 2). The

Table 2.   Structure of the economically active population according to sphere and sector of the economy and sex in the provinces studied, 1981 (percentages[a])

Sphere and sector	City of Havana		Cienfuegos		Guantánamo	
	Male	Female	Male	Female	Male	Female
Material sphere	64.4	44.6	77.3	48.1	74.8	45.9
Agriculture and forestry	2.3	1.3	32.3	14.1	37.7	19.8
Industry and construction	38.8	24.8	32.3	18.1	22.8	11.5
Communication and transport	12.4	4.6	7.2	3.4	6.9	3.2
Commerce	10.9	13.9	5.5	12.5	7.4	11.4
Non-material sphere	32.4	52.5	18.6	47.5	20.9	50.4
Not declared	3.2	2.9	4.1	4.4	4.3	3.8

[a] Totals may not add up exactly, owing to rounding.

Source: CEE (1983), Vols. II, III and VIII, table 50.

figures show how female participation is predominantly concentrated in the non-material sectors of the economy[1]. Less than half of the female labour force is in the material sectors of the economy in all three areas, whereas the majority of the male labour force is found in these sectors.

In addition, it may be observed that the female concentration in the non-material sphere is even greater where the population is more urbanised, as in the City of Havana. In Cienfuegos, on the other hand, although the proportion of working women in the non-material sphere is relatively high, the percentage in the agriculture and forestry sector is as high as 14.1 per cent, owing to the high level of agricultural development around the capital city. In Guantánamo, too, agriculture and forestry are of considerable importance to women, although a high proportion are absorbed by non-material activities. In this region women also play an important role during the tobacco harvest.

The employment structure of each area is a reflection of its economic activities. In Plaza de la Revolución are located the vast majority of the country's cultural and higher-level educational institutions such as the University of Havana, the oldest centre of higher education in Cuba, the headquarters of the main government bodies, and various large chain stores.

Cienfuegos, on the other hand, has benefited from several important industrial investments since the Revolution, including a large thermo-electric plant whose generation capacity has increased five times in only five years, a modern fertiliser plant, a fuel refinery, a shipping terminal for bulk sugar, and a highly sophisticated paper mill in addition to food production and light industry devoted to local consumption.

In Yateras, the economy is basically agricultural, apart from drying areas and processing plants for coffee, and a chain of retail stores which satisfy the increasing needs of its population. In fact, it was largely the development of the coffee industry which led to the construction of a main road of 42 kilometres connecting the main inhabited areas and the extension of the electricity service. Yateras, previously without electricity and separated from the capital of the province by a road only passable during the dry season, is today less than one hour's drive from the city of Guantánamo.

2.3 Education, health and living conditions

In the sphere of education, regional differences persist. In 1981, the population of Plaza de la Revolución and of its province had had, on average, 9.6 and 8.3 years of schooling respectively, while the populations of the provinces of

11

Cienfuegos and Guantánamo had had 6.6 and 5.5 years (see table 3). In spite of these unequal educational levels, however, in all the populations studied, important increases in educational levels had occurred during recent years, reflecting the expansion of secondary education between the censuses of 1953 and 1981.

However, if we analyse the proportion of the population aged 6 years and over registered in any level of education - that is the schooling rate - it will be found that this is highest for women in Guantánamo where the average level of schooling is lowest (table 4). This reflects the fact that the educational infrastructure is adapted to the stage of development that education has reached in the three areas. Thus the City of Havana has 71.3 classrooms for every 10,000 inhabitants aged 6 years and older, Cienfuegos has 79.0, and Guantánamo has 84.0^2 (CEE, 1981, pp. 22-28).

The more favourable treatment given to the province with the lowest average level of schooling with regard to the provision of educational resources is reflected not only in classroom facilities but also in teaching personnel. Thus, in Guantánamo, in the 1981 school year, there were 30.4 persons working in jobs related to teaching for every 1,000 members of the population aged 6 years and over, while in Cienfuegos and City of Havana this rate was 26.7 and 29.6 respectively (CEE, 1981, Vols. II, III and VIII, tables 49 and 38).

If one looks at the schooling rates of the population aged between 6 and 13 years of age there is in fact little difference between the different areas. Thus in 1981 the City of Havana had 98.3 per cent of children studying, while in Cienfuegos the percentage was 97.0 and in Guantánamo it is slightly lower at 95.1 (CEE, 1981, Vols. II, III and VIII, tables 49 and 47). In all three areas, the proportion of children that drop out of school is very low, and a lack of schools in the community or inadequate school capacity is practically never the reason for dropping out, even in the less urbanised regions[3]. Even in the most remote mountain regions of the country, where the population density is low and the dispersion of the population is high, the children attend school every day, wearing uniforms and shoes, just like the children of the capital city.

In terms of health and mother-and-child services, too, the provinces studied have very similar facilities, despite their very different levels of urbanisation. While the numbers of beds and medical consultations reveal some differences, owing to the concentration of more specialised medical units of national coverage in the capital, the other provinces studied do none the less have paediatric and maternal-infant hospitals, as well as rural hospitals which dispense basic and maternity services. The City of Havana, with 19.8 per cent of the country's total

12

Table 3. Changes in the structure of the population according to educational levels and average years of study, 1953 and 1981 (percentages)

Educational level and years of study	City of Havana		Cienfuegos		Guantánamo	
	1953	1981	1953	1981	1953	1981
Primary 6 years and less	75.7	46.8	90.2	62.0	92.9	60.3
General Secondary 7-12 years	21.0	46.1	9.2	36.0	6.8	37.7
Higher 13 years or more	3.3	7.1	0.6	2.0	0.3	2.0
	100.0	100.0	100.0	100.0	100.0	100.0
Average years of study	4.8	8.3	3.2	6.6	2.1	5.5

Source: CEE (1983), Vols. II, III and VIII, pp. xc, xciii and xci respectively.

13

Table 4. <u>Schooling rates by province of the population of 6</u> <u>years and over according to sex, 1981</u>[a] (percentages)

Province	Schooling rate		
	Total	Male	Female
City of Havana	37.8	59.8	35.5
Cienfuegos	37.4	38.5	36.1
Guantánamo	47.1	49.7	44.3

[a] This refers to the percentage of the population aged 6 years and over registered in study centres.

Source: CEE (1983), Vols. II, III and VIII, tables 41 and 47.

population in 1981, had eight paediatric hospitals and two maternal-infant hospitals, while Cienfuegos and Guantánamo (with 3.4 and 4.8 per cent respectively of the island's population) had two and four such hospitals respectively, though the rural mountain hospitals do differ to some extent from other hospitals[4]. In addition, in 1984, there were a total of 31 intensive care wards throughout the country, which contribute considerably to the saving of human lives, particularly those of infants.

If we look at the number of persons in the medical professions - that is, nurses, technicians and doctors - we can see that they are more numerous in the City of Havana (table 5). This is partly due to the demands of the national health administration itself, which is situated in the capital city.

The final result of health administration, expressed through the infant mortality rate, is not very different in the three provinces (table 5) and reflects the high level of health services even in remote areas. It can be noted that the infant mortality rate in Cuba as a whole is very low (17 per thousand in 1982) for a developing country, approaching that of industrial market economies which average about 10 per thousand (World Bank, 1984, table 230).

The types of housing and the presence of electricity and electrical goods, such as radios and televisions, reflect the different levels of economic development in the provinces under study, serving at the same time to illustrate the living conditions of women in these areas (table 6).

Table 5.   Selected health indicators in the provinces studied,
            1981

Health indicator	City of Havana	Cienfuegos	Guantanamo
Beds per 1,000 inhabitants	10.7	5.0	3.8
Consultations per 1,000 inhabitants	4.1	3.2	1.8
Health service employees per 1,000 inhabitants	16	9	7.0
Infant mortality rate (a)	15.9	16.4	21.6

(a) Deaths of children under 1 year old per thousand born
     alive.
Sources: Provincial Peoples Power, Divisions of Health: Infant
           mortality rates reported to the National Directorate
           of the FCW;   CEE (1983), Vols. II, III and VIII,
           table 49; MINSAP, n.d., p. 31, 34 and 15.

Table 6.   Some standard of living indicators in the provinces
            studied, 1981

Standard of living indicators	City of Havana	Cienfuegos	Guantanamo
Percentage of houses types I, II and III (a)	95	70	58
Percentage of houses with electricity (b)	99	80	65
Radios for every 100 houses with electricity	88	103	121
TV sets for every 100 houses with electricity	83	69	60

(a) This typology includes houses built with concrete, bricks,
     wooden walls and plates, with tiles or wooden roofs; it
     excludes houses with fibro-cement, metal or guano roofs and
     palm tree walls, characteristic of type IV.
(b) This refers to electrification from specialised state
     enterprises and from industrial or own plants.
Source: CEE (1983), Vols. II, III and VIII, graphs 14 and 15
           and tables 6 and 19.

The City of Havana thus shows the highest percentage of houses built of good-quality materials and with reasonable security. This percentage decreases as the area becomes more rural. Then the typical "bohío", a house built with guano roof and palm tree walls, tends to appear. Similarly, the percentage of houses with electricity is highest in the city of Havana and lowest in Guantánamo, a province whose rural population still represents 47 per cent of the total inhabitants.

The number of radios and television sets, which is calculated in relation to the total number of houses with electricity, suggests the presence of more equitable distribution criteria for these commodities. The territorial differences as far as this indicator is concerned are slight. In the provinces where the percentage of houses without electricity is larger, the number of radios per 100 houses with electricity is actually over 100, which points to the presence of battery-run radios where there is no electricity.

2.4 Demographic characteristics

Table 7 shows the total population and the intercensal net increase rate of the provinces and municipalities studied.

Table 7. Total population and intercensal net increase rate of the areas studied

Area of study	Population (thousands) 1981	Intercensal growth rate (%) 1970-81
Plaza de la Revolución	164.5	0.3
Cienfuegos	114.6	1.6
Yateras	21.7	-1.0
Province		
City of Havana	1 929.4	0.7
Cienfuegos	326.4	0.9
Guantánamo	466.0	1.0
Cuba	9 723.6	1.1

Source: CEE (1983), Vols. II, III and VIII, table 1.

The population of the municipality of Plaza de la Revolución represents 8 per cent of the population of the capital, while that of the municipality of Cienfuegos represents as much as 35 per cent of the population of the province of the same name. The population of Yateras, on the other hand, has very little quantitative significance within the total

16

provincial population and has been decreasing, despite higher fertility rates, probably because of a high level of emigration. The increasing population in the municipality of Cienfuegos can be explained by the large number of immigrants who are attracted by the socio-economic development that is taking place.

The population structure of the municipalities studied, according to three broad age groups, is shown in table 8. What is immediately revealed is a greater degree of ageing of the population in the municipalities of Plaza and Cienfuegos and their respective provinces. Both provinces have a low fertility rate and receive immigrants from other provinces, the majority of whom are adult workers. Guantánamo and Yateras show the lowest proportions of older people, which is indicative, of course, of a present and past fertility rate higher than that of the other areas. A more detailed analysis of the structure of the population by five-year age and sex groups (see Appendix 2) shows that the proportion of the population from 0 to 4 years old is highest in Yateras and lowest in Plaza.

Table 8. <u>Age distribution of the population in the areas studied (in percentages) and masculinity index[a], 1981</u>

Area of study	Age group			Masculinity index
	Under 15 years	15-64	65 and over	
Plaza de la Revolución	20.9	68.5	10.6	90.0
Cienfuegos	28.5	62.2	9.3	98.1
Yateras	43.4	52.5	4.1	115.1
Province				
City of Havana	24.2	66.2	9.6	91.9
Cienfuegos	29.4	62.0	8.6	105.0
Guantánamo	36.9	57.5	5.6	104.6

[a] Refers to males per 100 females.
Source: CEE (1983), Vols. II, III and IV, table 1.

The sex composition of the population shows the typical differences between urban and rural areas. As the level of urbanisation increases, so the masculinity index decreases, that is, the proportion of women increases. Thus, Yateras is the municipality with the lowest proportion of women, and Plaza de la Revolución that with the highest, with only just over nine men for every ten women.

The behaviour of the masculinity index (males per 100 females) by age group obtained in the last census is also presented in Appendix 2. It shows that in the municipality of Yateras men are predominant in all age groups. This situation may be a reflection of the migratory processes which have historically affected the development of its population. Amongst the older age groups the masculinity indices show up to 219 men for every 100 women, which suggests a particularly high level of female emigration during the second and third decades of this century. On the other hand, the values reached for the masculinity index, especially for the population 20 years old and over, in the municipalities of Plaza de la Revolución and Cienfuegos, are typical of those found in urban areas, where female immigration seems to be an important factor.

Appendix 3 compares the structure of the female population from 15 to 59 years old by age group in each municipality at the time of the 1981 census with that of the female population surveyed. Although the relative size of the sample, in terms of the percentage of the total female population that was surveyed, is different in each municipality[5], the figures given in Appendix 3 do confirm that the structure of the female population surveyed is very similar to that of the total female population of the municipalities.

The level of fertility, expressed through the crude birth rate (births per 1,000 population in a given year) as well as the general fertility rate and the gross reproduction rate, reveals that fertility is highest in Guantánamo. The values for the gross reproduction rates in the areas studied are shown in table 9 where it can be seen that, as the degree of urbanisation decreases, fertility increases.

Table 9. Gross reproduction rates for the areas of study, 1981

Area of study	Gross reproduction rate[a]
Plaza de la Revolución	0.59
Cienfuegos	0.80
Yateras	1.40
Province	
City of Havana	0.65
Cienfuegos	0.81
Guantánamo	1.05

[a] The gross reproduction rate is the average number of daughters a woman would bear if she experienced the age-specific fertility rates observed in a given year.

Source: Preliminary estimates elaborated by the authors from information provided by the Statistics State Committee and the Ministry of Public Health.

Plaza and Cienfuegos thus have lower fertility levels than their respective provinces, the populations of both municipalities having a higher average educational level and being more completely urbanised than the populations of the provinces as a whole. Yateras, by contrast, has a higher fertility rate than its own province, Guantánamo, corresponding to the lack of any urban population in its mountainous territory. Yateras and its province Guantánamo also show higher specific rates of fertility in each age group than the other areas under study.

The general mortality rate, by contrast, is less differentiated in the three areas of study, owing to the fairly uniform distribution of medical assistance and health services throughout Cuba. General death rates of 7.6 per thousand for City of Havana, and 6.0 and 4.5 per thousand for Cienfuegos and Guantanamo respectively[6], are quite similar, the differences reflecting the different proportion of older people in the three provinces.

The situation concerning migration is very different in the three areas, especially internal migration. Although external migration produces negative migratory balances throughout the country – and much more so in the province and City of Havana and its municipalities – it is internal migration which largely explains the dissimilarities in the demographic trends in the populations studied.

The City of Havana and the municipality of Plaza show positive internal migration rates of over 4 per cent[7] although this is low in comparison with the rates found for any of the more populous capitals of Latin America. Cienfuegos showed negative balances for more than a decade, but from 1979 these began to be reversed, and at present the province shows positive rates, although very low ones, thus indicating that internal immigration is now able to neutralise the effects of emigration.

Guantánamo Province, as a whole, has shown a negative internal migratory balance for more than four decades; at present its net migration rate is -7.4 per cent[8], its neighbouring province, Santiago de Cuba, being the chief place of destination for its migrants. The municipality of Yateras in its turn presents a still higher level of internal emigration, which can be explained by the scarcity both of basic services and of other resources such as recreational facilities and higher education which are now being demanded by a population whose average level of schooling has been raised.

*   *   *

For a country which is making strenuous efforts to overcome underdevelopment, the task of minimising the differences between regions at very different stages of development constitutes a formidable challenge. The data presented in this chapter show that the Government has made considerable progress in reducing former regional differences although small differences continue to exist.

Notes

[1] In socialist countries the two main branches of the economy are material and non-material production. Material production includes agriculture, industry, construction, transport, communication and trade, and the supply of technical material. Non-material production includes mainly services such as education, science, health and communal utilities and services. These are sometimes referred to as the productive and non-productive branches of the economy.

[2] These figures exclude classrooms for the teaching of adults and university studies, with which the City of Havana is obviously better provided, as the services it offers at this level of education go beyond the limits of its territory, being national in scope. However, both Guantánamo and Cienfuegos do have centres for higher education where they teach certain university courses.

[3] The 1981 census showed that in all the provinces under study, the proportion of the child population who did not attend school for these reasons was less than 12 per cent of the total of children not registered.

[4] Cienfuegos and Guantánamo provinces have four and eight rural mountain hospitals respectively.

[5] The female population surveyed represented approximately 20 per cent, 3 per cent and 2.5 per cent of the female population aged between 15 and 59 years of the municipalities of Yateras, Plaza and Cienfuegos respectively, bearing in mind that in the latter case the representativeness to be obtained was not at the level of the municipality of Cienfuegos, but only of one of its districts.

[6] Information supplied by the Dirección Nacional de Estadísticas del Ministerio de Salud Pública (National Statistics Bureau of the Ministry of Public Health) for 1981.

[7] The internal migration rates of the province have remained at this level, sometimes reaching a maximum value of 6.3 per cent, for the last 12 years, according to official statistics.

20

⁸ Migratory balance with respect to the median population of 1981, obtained from the Registry for Change of Domicile.

CHAPTER III

A PROFILE OF WOMEN IN THE AREAS STUDIED

In terms of the results obtained in the survey (EDEMU-82), the questions which seem best designed to characterise women in each of the areas of study, as well as the changes that have taken place between generations, will be discussed in this chapter. Among the elements dealt with are educational and cultural levels, participation in economic activity, position within the family group and conjugal problems.

3.1 Women's educational and cultural levels

As concerns the educational level of women in the three areas of study, the survey results have given a clear reflection of this expansion of education, above all among the youngest women, who have lived all or a great part of their life during the revolutionary period.

For the purpose of this study, the number of years of schooling was grouped in the following way:

Primary level	0-6
Basic medium level	7-9
Higher medium level	10-12
Higher or university level	13 and over

And in order to perceive the changes that have taken place between the different generations, the women interviewed in the three areas were divided into two age groups: women between 15 and 30 years old and women over 30 years of age.

Table 10 shows the educational level of the women according to these broad age groups. The figures point to two main areas of differentiation. The first is the generational change. In the younger age group, the proportion of women educated beyond primary level is substantially greater in all three regions. In Plaza de la Revolución, for instance, only 8.2 per cent of the younger generation had stopped their education at the primary level, while amongst the older women the figure was 41.9 per cent. It is thus obvious that the efforts made by the State since 1959, through the literacy campaign and subsequent educational programmes, have provided massively improved levels of education.

Table 10.　Percentage distribution of women according to
　　　　　educational level and broad age group

Area of study	Primary	Basic medium	Higher medium	University	TOTAL
Age group 15-29 years					
Plaza de la Revolución	8.2	42.7	41.7	7.4	100
Buenavista	32.0	44.7	20.7	2.6	100
Yateras	46.4	43.0	10.4	0.2	100
Age group 30 years and over					
Plaza de la Revolución	41.9	18.7	25.6	13.8	100
Buenavista	71.6	17.5	8.8	2.1	100
Yateras	83.0	15.3	1.5	0.2	100

Source:　EDEMU-82.

The second area of differentiation relates to the
socio-economic status of the three areas of study. The figures
show that educational levels improve as the degree of
urbanisation increases. Plaza de la Revolución thus presents
both the greatest degree of urbanisation and the highest levels
of education. It should however be remarked that migratory
trends are influencing these figures, since it is the more
educated who emigrate from Yateras and who immigrate to Plaza.
Nevertheless, even the figures for women currently living in
Yateras show that substantial improvement has taken place in
educational levels throughout the country.

Those interviewed were also asked questions about their
mothers, amongst other things about their educational level in
1959. Values for the educational level of the interviewees in
relation to that of their mothers were thus obtained (table 11).

In the extreme case of Yateras, almost all the mothers had
studied only the primary grades, while 37.6 per cent of the
daughters had reached a higher level of education. The
difference between mothers and daughters in the numbers reaching
the higher medium and university levels in Plaza de la
Revolución should also be noted.

Table 11. <u>Percentage distribution of women according to their educational level and that of their mothers</u>

Educational level	Plaza de la Revolución		Buenavista		Yateras	
	Mothers	Daughters	Mothers	Daughters	Mothers	Daughters
Primary	70.9	28.9	87.4	52.8	93.3	62.4
Basic medium	11.7	28.0	4.2	30.4	0.8	30.9
Higher medium	11.0	31.6	2.4	14.5	0.3	6.5
University	1.9	11.5	1.0	2.3	-	0.2
TOTAL	95.5[a]	100.0	95.0[a]	100.0	94.4[a]	100.0

[a] The total does not add up to 100 because some interviewees were unable to answer the question about their mother's schooling.

Source: EDEMU-82.

Concerning the average number of years of schooling, according to estimates made from the results of the survey, the women of Plaza de la Revolución had had an average of 9.6 years while the figures for Buenavista and Yateras were 7.4 and 6.1 per cent respectively. The results by age shown in figure 2 show that the younger women had reached significantly higher levels, especially in the semi-urban and rural areas[1].

In Yateras, the oldest women had had on average less than three years of schooling, while the young women had had over seven years. In Plaza de la Revolución the increase was from about seven years to more than ten. It can thus be seen that women in the three areas start from very different bases.

These figures confirm that in the urban as well as the rural areas a massive advance in women's education has been made. There are still regional differences, but these are less in the youngest age groups.

Self-improvement and further education

Also extremely important is the self-improvement and further education that a great many people undertake after attaining a certain educational level, as a means of bringing up to date and developing the knowledge acquired during full-time education. This refers to courses related to people's jobs, the furthering of technical knowledge, the study of music, literature, languages or politics, postgraduate courses, and so on.

Figure 2. Women's average years of study

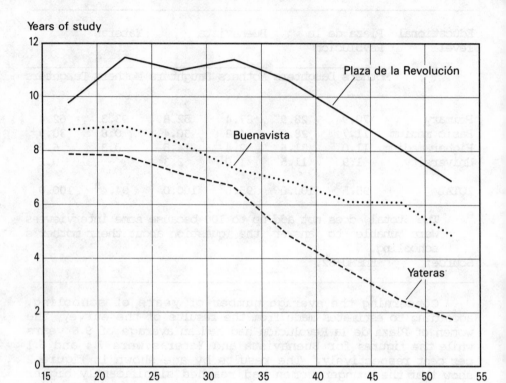

Source: EDEMU-82.

The interviewees were asked whether they had attended any courses of this kind since leaving school. Results are presented in table 12 so as to show the differences between two different generations.

Table 12. <u>Percentage of women who have attended self-improvement courses in broad age groups</u>

Age group	Plaza de la Revolución	Buenavista	Yateras
15-29	80.1	72.4	58.6
30 years and over	54.6	47.6	49.1

Source: EDEMU-82.

The higher values are found in the younger generation, naturally the one which has had greater opportunities. Nevertheless, in all three areas of study, roughly 50 per cent of women aged 30 years and over had attended some sort of self-improvement course, which is a fairly high proportion.

In many societies, women who are married or in a consensual union tend to have difficulty in continuing their studies and consequently in obtaining a higher educational level. In this respect, one of the most interesting findings of the survey was the percentage of women who were married or in a consensual union who reported that they were presently studying: 40, 33 and 37 per cent in Plaza de la Revolución, Buenavista and Yateras respectively (table 13).

Table 13. <u>Percentage of women who presently study according to conjugal situation</u>

Conjugal situation	Plaza de la Revolución	Buenavista	Yateras
Married or in consensual union	40.0	33.1	36.9
Widowed	4.4	3.5	5.6
Separated	21.9	31.0	18.2
Single	73.9	70.4	30.8
All women	31.53	28.79	18.81

Note: In each item in the table the complement to 100 is the proportion who do not study.

Source: EDEMU-82.

27

Amongst single women, however, the percentage was only 30.8 per cent in Yateras, while in Plaza de la Revolución and Buenavista the figures were 73.9 and 70.4 per cent respectively. This result merits particular attention from the social organisations that work in Yateras, among them the Federation of Cuban Women.

Contact with communications media

In order to assess to some extent the interest shown by the interviewees in their social environment, they were asked how often they read the newspapers, listened to the radio, watched television or read magazines and books. These elements were combined to create a compound indicator, which resulted in three alternative levels of contact with information sources: low, medium and high. A detailed explanation of this indicator is given in Appendix 4.

In all three study areas, the proportion of women with low media contact was greater among women aged 30 or more as compared to younger women (table 14). The younger women were able to take more interest in learning about the social reality which surrounded them, thus making possible a greater degree of participation in society and at the same time enriching the experiences which they can pass on to their children.

Table 14.   Percentage distribution of women according to degree of media contact and age group

Area	15-29 years				30 years and over			
	Low	Medium	High		Low	Medium	High	
Plaza de la Revolución	4.0	41.3	48.7	100.0	10.1	52.0	37.9	100.0
Buenavista	5.7	50.0	44.3	100.0	17.2	60.7	22.1	100.0
Yateras	22.9	60.0	17.1	100.0	46.3	46.3	7.4	100.0

Source: EDEMU-82.

The age difference is related to the higher educational levels of younger women. Table 15 shows that as educational levels increase, the percentage of women with low media contact declines. In Plaza de la Revolución, for example, the percentages are 17.9, 7.1, 2.0 and 0.0, corresponding to the primary, basic medium, higher medium and university levels respectively.

The preceding analysis shows the educational and cultural advances women have achieved in the last two decades. Such successes stand out in the younger generations, who have greatly surpassed their mothers and grandmothers, although favourable changes are also found in the latter.

Table 15.   Percentage distribution of women according to degree of media contact and educational level

Educational level	Area	Contact with media			Total
		Low	Medium	High	
Primary	Plaza de la				
	Revolución	17.9	61.2	20.9	100.0
	Buenavista	19.3	63.3	17.4	100.0
	Yateras	46.4	48.8	4.8	100.0
Basic medium	Plaza de la				
	Revolución	7.1	52.0	40.9	100.0
	Buenavista	3.6	50.4	46.0	100.0
	Yateras	12.7	67.0	20.3	100.0
Higher medium	Plaza de la				
	Revolución	2.0	46.6	51.4	100.0
	Buenavista	3.4	44.9	51.7	100.0
	Yateras	5.2	41.4	53.4	100.0
University	Plaza de la				
	Revolución	0	27.9	72.1	100.0
	Buenavista	0	15.8	84.2	100.0
	Yatera	0	15.8 [a]	84.2 [a]	100.0

[a] Non-representative values.

Source: EDEMU-82.

3.2 Women's participation in economic activity

In order to be able to compare the results obtained in the present survey with the information derived from the 1981 Census of Population and Dwellings, the questions (related to economic activities) were asked in the same manner as those in the census and the same categories of analysis are used. Thus the rates of economic participation derived from the survey are based on what women reported they were doing the preceding week (see Appendix 5 for details).

Activity rates

The economic activity rates of women calculated from the survey data correspond closely to those of the 1981 census except in the case of Yateras (table 16). The higher participation rate in the survey data for Yateras is because the survey was carried out during the month of October, which coincides with the harvesting of coffee. In this agricultural rural zone, women do contract work for short periods of time during the cultivation or crop seasons of the indigenous products.

The values for the three areas show a high rate of participation by women in economic activity, which represents an important contribution to the national economy. Participation rates are highest in Plaza de la Revolución.

Table 16. <u>Economic activity rates of women aged 15-59 according to the 1981 Census and the survey data (percentages)</u>

Area	Activity rate	
	1981 Census	EDEMU-82
Plaza de la Revolución	61.8	62.7
Buenavista	47.7[a]	48.4
Yateras	31.0	43.6

[a] The calculation was made for the municipality of Cienfuegos; Buenavista is registered as a district of this municipality.

Sources: EDEMU-82; CEE (1983) Vols. II, III and VIII, pp. CII, CIV and CVI.

In order to gain a more detailed picture of women's economic activity, seven possibilities with regard to activity status were considered, taking as a reference period the week before the day of the survey. The description of each of these possibilities appears in Appendix 5. The results obtained are summarised in table 17.

It will be noticed that the proportion of women working for money is high in all three areas and that most of the women included in the active population are in fact working, with very few unemployed.

Figure 3 shows the proportion of employed women according to age in the three areas. It is noticeable that in Buenavista women begin their working life at an earlier age than in Plaza de la Revolución: in the 15-19 age group, 19.2 per cent of women were active compared with 11.1 per cent in Plaza, where more young women continue to study.

Table 17. Percentage distribution of women aged 15-59 according to activity status[a]

Activity status	Plaza de la Revolución	Buenavista	Yateras
Active			
Working for money	59.7	45.5	40.7
Looking for a job because had resigned or lost it	1.0	1.4	0.4
First time looking for a job	2.0	1.5	2.5
Inactive			
Retired	2.1	0.6	2.0
Student	16.1	11.0	1.6
Housewife	17.1	32.9	41.8
Other situation	2.0	7.0	11.0
	100.0	100.0	100.0

[a] Totals may not add up exactly, owing to rounding.
Source: EDEMU-82.

In Yateras, as many as 23 per cent of 15-19 year old women are economically active, a level which has to do with the lower level of socio-economic development. In all three areas, women's participation rates initially increase as a function of age, remain relatively stable over several age groups, and then decline after the age of 45.

Amongst the inactive categories, that of housewife occurs most frequently in Yateras, at 41.8 per cent. In Buenavista the percentage decreases to 32.9 while in Plaza de la Revolución only 17.1 per cent of women devote themselves solely to housework. As has been seen, it is in this urban area that the highest proportion of women are employed, corresponding to the level of development reached. When analysing the percentage distribution by age of the housewives, it is found that the percentage increases among older women.

In the student category, the highest percentage (16.1) is found in Plaza de la Revolución. This result confirms that this is the area where women study for the greatest number of years. The number of women studying diminishes to 11.0 per cent in Buenavista while in Yateras only 1.6 per cent of women were full-time students. In Yateras, it should be borne in mind, marriage often takes place at an early age. This could partly explain both the low proportion of students and the high proportion of housewives.

Figure 3. Proportion of employed women according to age in the areas of study

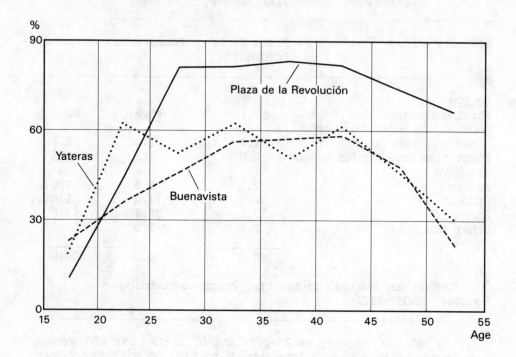

Source: EDEMU-82.

The age group where the percentage of students is highest is 15-19 years. In Plaza de la Revolución, for instance, nearly 80 per cent of women between those ages are students, though in Yateras the figure is less than 10 per cent. In Buenavista more than half of all women between 15 and 19 years old study as their basic activity.

This analysis reflects the socio-economic differentiation between the three areas. Plaza de la Revolución is an urban zone of the capital with a high level of development and therefore a variety of sources of employment. Women study longer than in the other zones and show greater interest in economic and cultural activities. The high level of labour force participation remains steady due to individual and socio-economic factors and to a better understanding of the role of women in society. The same tendencies are present in Buenavista and Yateras, but less markedly.

Occupational category

Employed women were asked about the work they performed, which was classified into seven occupational categories. These are the same as those in the questionnaire used in the Population and Dwellings Census of 1981 (see details in Appendix 6). Table 18 shows the proportion of women in each occupational category.

Table 18. <u>Percentage distribution of women according to occupation</u>[a]

Occupational category	Plaza de la Revolución	Buenavista	Yateras
Executives	4.5	5.2	1.4
Professionals and technicians	47.2	33.4	21.8
Administrative workers	18.3	17.8	9.5
Service workers	19.6	28.2	35.4
Agricultural workers	0.1	3.7	28.3
Non-agricultural workers	8.5	11.7	2.4
Others	1.8	–	1.1
	100.0	100.0	100.0

[a] Totals may not add up exactly, owing to rounding

Source: EDEMU-82.

In both Plaza de la Revolución and Buenavista the category which groups the highest number of women is that of professionals and technicians, 47.2 and 33.4 per cent respectively - a result which is directly related to the educational levels reached by the female population in these areas and to the types of employment available to them.

The next most important category is that of service workers. This is particularly true of the suburban area of Buenavista, where 28.2 per cent of the female labour force is located in this sector. In Plaza de la Revolución the percentage for service workers is similar to that for administrative workers, 19.6 and 18.3 per cent respectively.

In Yateras, unlike the other two areas, the most important category is service workers, which absorbs 35.4 per cent of the female labour force. Here again, this is directly related to educational levels and opportunities in the area.

As Yateras is a rural zone, it is not surprising that 28.3 per cent of women workers should be grouped in the "agricultural workers" category. The proportion of women who fall into the "professionals and technicians" category is nevertheless high: one working woman out of every five. This can be explained if one bears in mind the relatively high level of educational and health services, sectors in which women tend to play an important part.

The lowest percentage overall is that for the category of executives - a result which emphasises the need to continue the work now being done by the State to increase the proportion of women in this category as one aspect of the campaign for the full equality of women.

In order to give some appreciation of the changes that have taken place during recent years in the distribution of women among the different occupational categories, table 19 compares the occupations of the interviewees with those of their mothers.

In all three areas it can be seen that the daughters are better represented in the higher occupational categories than their mothers. To take for example the professionals and technicians category: in Plaza de la Revolución, 47.2 per cent of the daughters fall into this category, but only 20.4 per cent of the mothers. In Buenavista the figure is three times higher for the daughters than for the mothers, 33.4 and 11.5 per cent respectively. In Yateras the increase between generations is still more significant: the figure is as low as 0.9 per cent for the mothers, rising to 21.8 per cent for the daughters. Even though this percentage is lower in Yateras, it is obviously a good start, given that this category was almost non-existent previously.

Table 19. Percentage distribution of women and their mothers, according to occupational category

Occupational category	Plaza de la Revolución		Buenavista		Yateras	
	Daughters	Mothers	Daughters	Mothers	Daughters	Mothers
Executives	4.5	0.4	5.2	-	1.4	-
Professionals and technicians	47.2	20.4	33.4	11.5	21.8	0.9
Administrative workers	18.3	7.7	17.8	-	9.5	-
Service workers	19.6	15.8	28.2	18.0	35.4	9.1
Agricultural workers	0.1	1.8	3.7	1.3	28.3	63.7
Non-agricultural workers	8.5	20.4	11.7	7.7	2.4	1.8
Personal services[a]	-	31.1	-	61.5	22.7	-
Others	1.8	1.8	-	-	0.9	-
Don't know/ Not available	-	0.4	-	-	1.1	0.9
TOTAL	100.0	100.0	100.0	100.0	100.0	100.0

a   This category had to be included to classify the mothers, owing to the large number of women who were domestic servants before the Revolution in 1959.

Source: EDEMU-82.

In the personal services category, too, a dramatic change has taken place, especially in Plaza de la Revolución and Buenavista where the values are 31.3 and 61.5 per cent, respectively, for the mothers. There are no registered values for the daughters. The personal services category has been disappearing as women attain higher educational levels, which enable them to work in jobs demanding higher qualifications.

In Yateras the largest category among the mothers is that of agricultural workers, this being for many of them one of the few ways of surviving in a period of labour surplus. Only 28.3 per cent of the daughters work in agriculture. Many of them have found occupations in the various facilities that have been established in recent years: schools, health services, workers' canteens, and so on.

Participation in political and mass organisations is an effective way of incorporating women into the community life of the country. The interviewees were asked whether they participated in voluntary activities such as the Movement of Militant Mothers for Education (see Chapter I), and the answers are shown in table 20.

Table 20. Proportion of women with responsibilities in political and mass organisations, according to age group

Age	Plaza de la Revolución	Buenavista	Yateras
15-19	45.1	43.7	30.3
20-24	53.8	43.5	43.8
25-29	40.6	49.5	44.7
30-34	44.9	56.4	50.4
35-39	45.0	41.4	37.9
40-44	49.5	52.9	32.7
45-49	42.0	59.5	16.0
50-54	40.1	40.0	7.0
55 and over	25.9	25.0	10.3
All women	43.8	47.1	31.2

Source: EDEMU-82.

According to the data, the proportion of women with concrete responsibilities in some organisation is high: in Plaza de la Revolución, over four out of ten women, in Buenavista almost half the women surveyed, and in Yateras three out of every ten women.

The behaviour of the different age groups is fairly similar in the three areas up to the age of 35. From this age, however, while the women of Plaza and Buenavista carry on in much the same way, the women of Yateras significantly reduce their participation in political and mass organisations. This corresponds with the age patterns of participation in economic activity, as seen above.

3.3 Family patterns and the situation of women

Another objective of this research was to study women within the family context. To this end, attention was focused on the more representative aspects of the household of which the interviewee was part, such as standard of living, number of family members, conjugal relationship, and so on. The aim here was to see how women's immediate family environment affects the way they behave in the wider society.

With the purpose of having a measure which allows us to compare families in the three areas, a compound standard of living indicator was created which includes average educational level of the household, per capital income and possession of durable items of equipment.

A detailed explanation of the indicator is given in Appendix 7. The standard of living indicator was used to classify families into four alternative groups, families with a standard of living that is high, medium, low or not calculable (in the case of not being able to obtain the information relating to one or more of the three components of the indicator).

Table 21 shows that the number of families with a low standard of living decreases as the degree of urbanisation

Table 21. Percentage distribution of sample women according to standard of living

Standard of living indicator [a]	Plaza de la Revolución	Buenavista	Yateras
Low	3.2	16.8	39.4
Medium	56.8	73.1	59.7
High	39.9	10.1	0.7
Not calculable	0.1	-	0.2
	100.0	100.0	100.0

[a] For the measurement of this indicator, see Appendix 7.
Source: EDEMU-82.

increases. In Yateras, they represent 39.4 per cent of the total while in Plaza de la Revolución they are only 3.2 per cent. In Buenavista, an intermediate zone, the figure is 16.8 per cent. The opposite is true of families with a high standard of living; they are least numerous in Yateras, while in Buenavista and Plaza de la Revolución the percentage increases.

The values obtained for the medium standard of living are also significant: in all three places more than 50 per cent of families came into this category. This result is consistent with the Government's aim of equalising the standard of living of the population and reducing the differences progressively.

Size and type of household

With regard to the size of the household of which the interviewee was part, the results show that in the rural zone it tends to be largest and in Plaza de la Revolución smallest (table 22). In Yateras, 44.1 per cent of interviewees lived in households with seven or more members as compared to 14.4 per cent in Plaza de la Revolución. According to the calculations made, the average size of household in Plaza de la Revolución, Buenavista and Yateras is 3.8, 4.7 and 5.6 people respectively.

Household size has a direct relationship with levels of fertility in each of these areas, as will be appreciated in the following chapters.

Table 22. Percentage distribution of sample women according to size of household

Number of persons in household	Plaza de la Revolución	Buenavista	Yateras
1-3	32.5	17.9	11.9
4-6	51.4	52.3	43.8
7 and more	14.4	29.5	44.1
Don't know	1.7	0.3	0.2
Total	100.0	100.0	100.0

Source: EDEMU-82.

Characteristics of heads of household

According to calculations made on the basis of the statements of the interviewees, the average age of heads of household is between 40 and 50 years in the three areas. For the purpose of comparison, table 23 also gives the figure for

Cuba as a whole. As the table shows, the results obtained in the survey on the average age of heads of household are very similar to those found for the population as a whole.

Table 23. <u>Average age of heads of household by sex in Cuba and in survey areas</u>

Sex	Cuba[a]	Plaza de la Revolución	Buenavista	Yateras
Female	49.2	50.2	46.5	41.3
Male	51.0	50.4	46.3	43.0

[a] 1979 figures.

Source: CEE, 1982, tables 1 and 9. EDEMU-82.

Conjugal situation

Women in the three areas of study tend to enter into conjugal relations (i.e. including marriage and consensual unions) at different ages, economic, educational and cultural factors all playing a part here.

The average age at which women enter their first conjugal relationship for Plaza de la Revolución, Buenavista and Yateras are 20.8, 18.9 and 18.4 years respectively. Women in the rural areas thus tend to enter conjugal relationships younger. However, what is considered the ideal age is more than two years older than the actual age in each case: 23.2, 22.5 and 21.7.

Table 24 analyses the survey data with regard to the conjugal status of the women. It can be seen that there are more single women in the urban areas, a result which is linked with the greater participation of urban women in education and subsequently in economic activity. In Plaza de la Revolución, single women thus amount to 23.6 per cent of the total, while in Buenavista and Yateras the figures are 17.4 and 11.6 per cent respectively.

According to the data, the highest percentage of married women is to be found in Buenavista (53.1 per cent) followed by Plaza de la Revolución (46.2 per cent) and Yateras (only 21.8 per cent). Here, women enter into conjugal relations younger but do not go through the official marriage ceremony as they do in the other two areas.

As concerns women in a consensual union - that is, those who maintain a not legalised but stable relationship with a partner - the highest percentage is found in Yateras (52.1 per cent),

Table 24. Percentage distribution of women according to
conjugal status

Conjugal status	Plaza de la Revolución	Buenavista	Yateras
Single	23.6	17.4	11.6
Married	46.2	53.1	21.8
Consensual union	7.9	16.3	52.1
Divorced or separated	19.4	10.7	12.4
Widowed	2.9	2.5	2.1
Total	100.0	100.0	100.0

Source: EDEMU-82.

and this proportion decreases as the level of urbanisation increases.

It should be noticed that if the married women and women in a consensual union are grouped together, then the highest proportion is obtained in Yateras (73.9 per cent). The figure is lower for Buenavista (69.4 per cent) and lower still for Plaza de la Revolución, where the married women and women in a consensual union together represent only 54.1 per cent of all women.

The figures for separated or divorced women are high, the highest being found in Plaza de la Revolución (19.4 per cent), where almost one out of every five women is divorced or separated. This result is related to generally greater participation of urban women in society which makes possible a greater degree of economic independence. It should be borne in mind that many people still hold reactionary views about women which conflict with the ideal of equality between men and women, and that in many cases this can create conflict between the couple. This, together with the fact that women, unlike in former times, can, with the support of the State, provide for their personal and family economic needs, goes a good way towards explaining this high rate of divorce. This is a logical transitional process.

Conjugal problems

Interviewees were asked about the problems in their present conjugal relationship. In Plaza de la Revolución, 47.3 per cent of the women in unions reported problems, in Buenavista, 42.6 per cent and in Yateras, 50 per cent. In order to ascertain which problems occurred most frequently, all the women who said they had problems (at least one) were taken, and the problems they reported were placed in order of importance for each area of study (see table 25).

In Plaza de la Revolución and Buenavista, the problems reported most frequently concern the lack of participation by the husband in child care and housework. Taken together, these amount to roughly 72.0 per cent of the problems most commonly reported.

The third most frequent conjugal difficulty in Plaza de la Revolución and Buenavista is infidelity, reported by 22.1 and 25 per cent respectively of the women with problems. In Yateras, this is the most frequent problem, reported by 50 per cent of the women.

Table 25. Proportion of women with most frequent conjugal problems

Conjugal problem	Plaza de la Revolución		Buenavista		Yateras	
	Rank	%	Rank	%	Rank	%
Her husband or mate does not take part in child care	1	36.8	2	30.4	4	20.1
Her husband or mate does not take part in housework	2	34.7	1	41.7	2	39.6
Her husband or mate is unfaithful	3	22.1	3	25.0	1	50.0
Differences in temperament	4	21.3	4	18.8	5	15.7
Housing problems	5	13.7	6	14.1	6	3.6
Her husband or mate drinks frequently	6	11.6	5	16.0	3	26.0

Source: EDEMU-82.

Frequent drinking is more of a problem in Yateras than in Plaza or Buenavista - a finding which can be explained by the relatively limited recreational facilities that exist in a rural area.

The conjugal problems that were detected are directly due to customs and habits that are difficult to change. Although some transformation has taken place, there is still some subordination of women to men in the conjugal relationship, which makes it impossible to establish true equality between the spouses. Inequality in the relationship of the couple is, particularly in the city, a common cause of divorce or separation.

Domestic burden

To gain an idea of how domestic tasks are distributed, the married women and women in a consensual union were asked about tasks carried out by them and their spouses.

From the answers was derived an indicator of "domestic burden". A numerical estimate was thus obtained, which resulted in four alternative groups. "Total or greater burden" means that the woman does most of the domestic tasks. "Slightly greater" means that the man co-operates to some extent with the woman. "Slightly less" means that women do less domestic work than their spouses. "None or less" means that most of the domestic work is done by the man. The relative values which resulted for these four groups are shown in table 26.

Table 26. Proportion of the domestic burden borne by women

Area	Total or greater	Slightly greater	Slightly less	None or less
Plaza de la Revolución	81.6	14.5	2.8	1.1
Buenavista	83.8	13.2	2.6	0.4
Yateras	95.8	3.1	0.8	0.3

Source: EDEMU-82.

From these results, it is obvious that most of the burden of work in the house is borne by women. This is even more marked in the rural zone where fewer women are involved in study and work outside the home, which means that their principal function is more likely to be running the household. But even in the capital the percentage of women who carry most of the burden is very high, taking into account that a great many of them study and/or are employed. In fact this "domestic burden" often constitutes a real obstacle to women's taking a decision-making role, both in the workplace and in political life, and even to their general incorporation into the economic, political and social life of the country.

Note

[1] It must be taken into account that in the recompilation of the information which gives rise to these results, it is understood that a person has reached a certain level when she has completely finished, and she may be studying the subsequent level without being counted in that level; for example, a girl studying in the ninth grade is considered to have finished only the primary level, as she has not finished studying the secondary level (nine years of studies). Thus schooling is in fact being underestimated.

CHAPTER IV

FERTILITY IN THE SURVEY AREAS

One of the aims of this work is to study fertility in relation to changes in the status of women. In this chapter, various fertility estimates from the current survey are compared with earlier data for the areas, in order to analyse the changes that have occurred and how these are related to women's educational levels, their participation in economic activity and their standard of living.

4.1 Fertility levels and trends

The surveys made by the Ministry of Public Health (MINSAP) in the areas of Plaza de la Revolución (September 1971) and Yateras (December 1972) allow us to compare the average number of children per woman to give us some idea of the evolution of fertility over a decade. As is known, this indicator presents various difficulties: among others, it is influenced, at the moment of making a comparison, by the different age structures of the populations surveyed. It must be borne in mind that the results express the historic reproductive experience of different groups of women throughout their life and not the present situation. In the case of Cuba, where it has already been mentioned that fertility levels have declined markedly during the last few years, particularly for women over 30, the indicator presents serious difficulties from the point of view of comparisons; however, it is useful to see these first results.

The information given in table 27 shows the changes that have taken place in a period of about ten years in the average number of children born per woman. On the one hand, it is interesting to observe how the changes in Plaza de la Revolución have not been as substantial, because the fertility levels were already low. The change that has taken place in Yateras, on the other hand, which is one of the areas with the highest fertility in the country, is significant, and substantially reduces the differential with Plaza de la Revolución: the average number of children in Yateras was 2.6 times higher than in Plaza in 1971, and only 2.1 times higher in 1982.

Another interesting finding is that the fertility of women from 15 to 19 years old has increased in Yateras, while in Plaza de la Revolución fertility in this age group is low and almost constant. This may be connected with differences in the age of marriage, as will be discussed later.

Table 27.   Estimated average number of children born alive per woman according to age group and different surveys

| Age group | Plaza de la Revolución | | Buenavista | Yateras | |
	MINSAP[a] (1971)	EDEMU (1982)	EDEMU (1982)	MINSAP[a] (1972)	EDEMU (1982)
15-19	0.09	0.07	0.16	0.35	0.42
20-24	0.79	0.34	0.85	2.00	1.23
25-29	1.25	1.02	1.63	3.84	2.46
30-34	2.00	1.60	2.41	5.75	3.27
35-39	2.02	1.92	2.92	7.17	4.57
40-44	2.27	2.25	3.37	8.11	6.05
45-49	2.00	2.42	3.90	8.95	7.30
15-49	1.58	1.29	1.85	4.17[b]	2.66

[a] Ministry of Public Health.
[b] Including 50 years.

Sources: EDEMU-82; Alvarez, 1982, table 31, p. 171.

The data relating to the average number of children per woman, together with information about births in the last year, allow us to estimate age-specific fertility rates (table 28). There are several methods of doing this (Mortara, 1948; Brass, 1974). After making some adjustments in fertility curves which were straying from the traditional patterns, it was possible to arrange these rates, as well as other fertility measures.[1]

The analysis of the age-specific fertility rates given in table 28 presents some interesting angles. Starting with Plaza de la Revolución, it can be affirmed that although fertility noticeably decreased in all age groups, the relative weight of fertility in the 15-19 age group remains almost the same - around 11 per cent. On the other hand, women 30 years old and over have made a disproportionate contribution to the overall decrease: while in 1971 they provided 34.2 per cent of the total fertility, in 1982 this value was 27.8.

The most significant finding is offered by Yateras, however: despite a slight reduction in the fertility rates of the 15-19 age group, the proportion they represent in relation to the total fertility increased from 11.2 per cent in 1972 to 22.5 per cent in 1982. This group of women thus occupies an increasingly important place in the contribution to fertility. In 1982 it registered a higher rate than women from 25 to 29 years old. In 1972, the contribution to the total fertility of women 30 years of age and more was 44.1 per cent, but by 1982 this had dropped to only 21.8 per cent; the age-specific rates for these women have therefore declined enormously.

Table 28. Estimated age-specific fertility rates and other fertility indicators according to different surveys

| Age group | Age-specific fertility (children per mother) | | | | |
| | Plaza de la Revolución | | Buenavista | Yateras | |
	MINSAP (1971)	EDEMU (1982)	EDEMU (1982)	MINSAP (1972)	EDEMU (1982)
15-19	0.057	0.026	0.053	0.169	0.156
20-24	0.159	0.080	0.147	0.342	0.237
25-29	0.120	0.065	0.077	0.298	0.148
30-34	0.097	0.036	0.045	0.270	0.077
35-39	0.064	0.019	0.028	0.204	0.044
40-44	0.014	0.008	0.017	0.122	0.025
45-49	0.000	0.004	0.005	0.042	0.006
Total fertility rate	2.6	1.2	1.9	7.2	3.5
General fertility rate	80.3	32.2	59.4	228.2	131.0
Crude birth rate	–	9.3	15.6	–	26.5

Sources: Computed from EDEMU-82, table 274, and Alvarez, 1982, tables 37 and 30, pp. 177 and 170.

It has been said that the eastern zone of the country has had a lot to do with the vertiginous decline in fertility experienced in Cuba over the last ten years. An example of this is provided by Yateras.

In Plaza de la Revolución, the age of maximum fertility, or the peak age of fertility, was 20-24 years: in both periods, an early peak. By 1982, however, the fertility of women from 25 to 29 years had increased its relative weight from 23.5 to 27.4 per cent. This indicates that fertility is tending towards an expanded peak.

Yateras presents a different situation: in 1972 fertility showed an early peak, but the fertility rates of women from 25

Figure 4. Fertility rates according to age and area, 1982

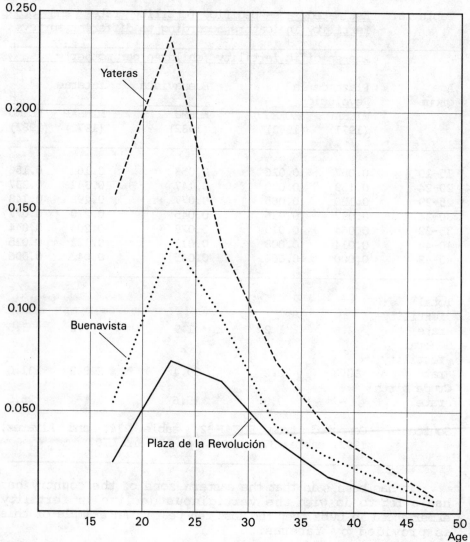

Age-specific fertility rate (children per woman)

Yateras

Buenavista

Plaza de la Revolución

Source: Table 28.

48

to 29 years old were very close to those of the 20-24 age group. By 1982, the fertility of this latter group accounted for 34.2 per cent of the total fertility, as compared with only 23.6 in 1972. Here it is worth repeating the hypothesis previously mentioned about the early age of conjugal union in this area of the country. Figure 4 presents the age-specific fertility rate curves and can also be used as a framework for comparing fertility in the three areas.

The relative increase in fertility in the younger age groups also becomes obvious if the mean age of fertility is taken into account, that is to say, the mean age of women who have children. In Plaza de la Revolución in 1971 this mean age was 27.4 years, but in 1982 it had decreased to 27.1 years. In Yateras the change is far more striking, the mean age dropping from 29.3 years in 1971 to only 25.4 in 1982. Buenavista occupies an intermediate position with respect to urbanisation; although its fertility levels are much closer to those of Plaza de la Revolución than to those of Yateras, its mean age of fertility is 26.4 years, that is, an intermediate position.

The estimated total fertility rates for the areas under study are indicative not only of the drastic reduction in fertility overall but also of the greatly reduced differences between the different areas. In 1972, the total fertility rate in Yateras surpassed that of Plaza de la Revolución by 4.6 children per woman. In 1982, however, the Yateras rate was only 2.3 children per woman higher than that of Plaza de la Revolución.

If we look at the total fertility rate for Plaza de la Revolución, probably the area of lowest fertility in the whole of Cuba, the figure of 1.2 children per woman is extremely low. It should be borne in mind that the lowest value reported in 1979 was 1.4 in the Federal Republic of Germany. Switzerland in that same year showed a value of 1.5; the Netherlands, 1.6; Sweden, 1.7; Bulgaria, 2.1; and Czechoslovakia, 2.3; all these countries are considered to have very low fertility levels (Haub, 1981). Even taking into consideration the fact that these last figures relate to whole countries while that from Plaza de la Revolución relates to a totally urbanised area, part of the capital city, the comparison is still remarkable.

The changes which have taken place in Cuban fertility, and which have been analysed using the vital statistics and other sources, such as the results of the current survey, are associated both with demographic and non-demographic factors. We will now examine some of these non-demographic factors.

4.2 Education and fertility

The previous chapter documented the great step forward that

49

has been made in education in Cuba in general, particularly for women. To what extent can the fact that Cuban fertility has declined rapidly in recent years be related to increasing levels of education?

The three areas which have been chosen for the survey reflect these changes, although showing some differences within the general framework of the country. The indicator used to estimate levels of fertility was the total fertility rate. As present estimation methods used were similar for all three areas and for all educational levels, the comparisons should be valid among themselves.[2]

What was found was that fertility levels decrease both as the degree of urbanisation increases and as educational levels increase (table 29).

Table 29. Estimation of the total fertility rate (children per woman) according to educational level

Educational level	Area			
	Plaza de la Revolución	Buenavista	Yateras	Cuba (1977)
Primary	2.8	3.4	3.9	3.1[a]
Basic medium	1.1	2.3	3.0	2.0
Higher medium	1.0	1.6	b	1.6
University	b	b	b	1.5

[a] Average of the values given in the different sources.
[b] The frequency of births was too low for a value to be estimated, but it is believed to be low.

Sources: EDEMU-82; CEE and CELADE, 1981, table 12.

Because of the small number of births in the previous year, the rates for the highest educational level were not calculated: in Plaza de la Revolución, for example, the 163 women of that educational level aged between 20 and 49 years had given birth to only three children in the year before the survey. At the other extreme are Yateras women with primary education only, whose total fertility rate is 3.9. However, even this level is still relatively low for a rural area of a developing country.

In order to compare 1982 fertility levels in the three areas with those of previous times, an estimation of the "average number of children per woman from 15 to 49 years" was made since this was the indicator used in surveys made by the Ministry of Public Health in the areas of Plaza de la Revolución and Yateras in the early 1970s (Alvarez, 1982; Alvarez, n.d.). As noted above, this measure presents several difficulties; however, it is useful as an indicator. Table 30 presents the results.

If we take the averages, without taking into account educational levels, the figures confirm yet again that fertility levels have decreased, particularly in Yateras, where they were previously higher. Standardising for educational level, however, the results do not show the declines expected within each level. Thus, it would appear that the overall fertility decline is due to the increasing numbers of women at higher educational levels where fertility tends to be less.

Table 30. <u>Average number of children born alive per woman from 15 to 49 years according to educational level and different surveys</u>

Educational level	Plaza de la Revolución[a]		Buenavista	Yateras	
	MINSAP (1971)	EDEMU (1982)	EDEMU (1982)	MINSAP (1972)	EDEMU (1982)
Primary		2.60	2.78		3.58
Grade 3 or less	2.43			6.32	
Grades 4 to 6	2.08			2.12	
Basic medium		1.54	0.97		1.42
Medium	1.48			0.86	
Higher medium		1.15	0.93		0.84
Higher		1.15	b		b
University	1.05			b	
All women	1.81	1.62	1.85	4.17	2.66

a   Women from 20 to 49 years.
b   Information non-existent or unreliable.

Sources: EDEMU-82; Alvarez and Ruben, 1973, table 9, p. 22; Alvarez, n.d., table 29, p. 48.

As regards differences between the areas surveyed in 1982, the trend at the primary level seems coherent, but not those at the basic medium and higher medium levels. When compared with MINSAP, the results are in several cases actually contradictory. The authors believe that these are the limitations of the indicator used.

The results given in table 30 show that there are still

different reproductive patterns both at the different educational levels and in the three areas surveyed; however, these regional differences are declining with rising educational levels.

In the future, the educational level of the 15-49 age group will continue to rise as the new generations displace the older generations who did not have the present opportunities. Consequently, some further reduction in reproductive levels can be expected, although not as great as in recent years.

4.3 Women's participation in economic activity and fertility

As seen in Chapter II, the situation of women in Cuba has been changing not only in terms of education but also with respect to their participation in economic activity. Many studies in several Latin American countries have shown an inverse relation between women's economic participation and fertility levels, though there are many different theories as to which factors determine this inverse relationship[3].

In the case of Cuba, the analysis of this relationship is particularly important. Over the last ten years, while women's economic participation has almost doubled - women of 14 years or older had a participation rate of 17.8 per cent in 1970 and 31.9 per cent in 1979 - fertility has declined to a little over half its former level.

With the purpose of making a deeper study of this relationship between women's economic participation and fertility, the labour situation of all the women interviewed was investigated using the same procedure as the last population census. In this way we it was possible to study, for each area, the fertility of women who were working for money and those who were not during the week before the interview.

In order to see what changes have taken place, the results were compared with those in two surveys made by the Ministry of Public Health (MINSAP) in 1971 and 1972, in the areas of Plaza de la Revolución and Yateras respectively.[4] The comparison is shown in table 31.

In table 31, the decrease in fertility is obvious for all groups apart from working women in Plaza de la Revolución. In Yateras, the higher number of children born to those who were working may be explained by the fact that the survey took place during the coffee harvest, when many women work temporarily. According to EDEMU-82 fertility levels in Plaza de la Revolución appear to be the same for both groups. This can be explained by the different age structure of the two groups of women: those who are between 20 and 24 years old and do not work - mostly because they are studying - represent one-third of the total of

Table 31. Mean number of children born alive per woman aged 20 to 49 years according to labour situation and different surveys

Labour situation and area	MINSAP (1971-72)	EDEMU (1982)
Plaza de la Revolución		
Working for money	1.6	1.6
Not working	2.0	1.6
Yateras		
Working for money	4.0	3.4
Not working	4.5	3.1

Sources: Alvarez and Ruben, 1973, table 11, p. 24. Alvarez, n.d., table 33, p. 52. EDEMU-82.

women; while those who are working in this group represent only 12 per cent. In fact, if the 20-24 age group is removed from the calculations, the average number of children per woman in Plaza de la Revolución is 1.8 for those who are working and 2.3 for those who are not.

Estimates of the present level of fertility (total fertility rate) in the three areas and according to the labour situation of women - that is, according to whether they were or were not working for money the week before the interview - are shown in table 32 and present a more clear-cut picture.[5]

Table 32. Estimated total fertility rate by labour situation

Area	Working	Not working	All women
Plaza de la Revolución	1.06	1.63	1.19
Buenavista	1.69	2.13	1.86
Yateras	2.69	4.14	3.47

Source: EDEMU-82.

The estimates of present fertility levels for the three areas show the expected very low levels in the most urban area (Plaza de la Revolución), intermediate levels in the semi-urban area (Buenavista), and relatively high levels in the rural area (Yateras). This difference is apparent in the total fertility rate for both working women and non-working women.

On the other hand, the fertility level of working women is lower than that of non-working women in all three areas. This differential is relatively similar in Plaza de la Revolución and Buenavista, but increases noticeably in Yateras. Here, the estimated fertility levels are always at least 50 per cent higher than those for the other two areas and in the case of women who do not work the figure is almost double.

The occupational category of women who worked the week before the interview was also investigated, using the same occupational classifications as in the last census. The women were then grouped into three broad occupational categories: Managerial, professional, and technical workers (Group I); administrative and service workers (Group II); and agricultural and non-agricultural workers (Group III). It was not possible to estimate the total fertility rate by occupational group because of the small number of women in each group who had had children the previous year, so table 33 shows the average number of children per woman.

In Plaza de la Revolución, as was to be expected, the lowest fertility levels were obtained for all three occupational groups. The difference between Group I and Group III is only 0.9 children per woman.

In Buenavista, an intermediate fertility level was obtained for the three occupational groups and the difference between Groups I and III amounted to 1.4 children per woman. In Yateras, by contrast, the difference between I and III amounted to 3.7 children per woman. It is important to underline that the composition by occupational group is different in the three areas. In Plaza de la Revolución, 55.1 per cent of the women belong to Group I, so it is the members of this group who basically determine the fertility level. In Buenavista and Yateras, on the other hand, Group II is dominant, with 45.2 and 48.9 per cent respectively, while Group III is also of considerable importance, especially in Yateras. For this reason fertility levels in these two areas, particularly Yateras, are determined by the women of these two occupational groups.

In Group I, the differences between fertility levels in the three areas are small. In Groups II and III, however, the differences between Plaza de la Revolución and Yateras are 1.2 and 3.0 children per woman, respectively.

The differentials by occupational group of women in the three areas may, however, be due to the nature of the indicator used, since older women are more likely to be in Group III occupations. This gives us some reason for thinking that differentials must have decreased, taking into account the fact that the reduction in fertility has taken place, above all, in women over 30 years old. In spite of this, the truth is that

Table 33. Average number of children per woman aged 20 to 49 years, according to occupational group

Occupational group	Plaza de la Revolución		Buenavista		Yateras	
	%[a]	Children per woman	%[a]	Children per woman	%[a]	Children per woman
I Managerial, professional and technical workers	55.1	1.3	39.6	1.4	21.7	1.5
II Administrative and service workers	36.0	2.0	45.2	2.6	48.9	3.2
III Agricultural and non-agricultural workers	7.2	2.2	15.2	2.8	28.2	5.2
IV Others	1.7	b	0.0	0.0	1.2	b
Total	100.0	1.6	100.0	2.2	100.0	3.4

a   Relative weight of women in each group.
b   The frequency is too low to be representative.

Source: EDEMU-82.

these differentials seem to be confirmed by the information obtained in EDEMU-82, though they may be smaller.

The information on the fertility of working and non-working women has confirmed the hypothesis that women currently working tend to have fewer children than those not working, although the direction of any causal link cannot be stated.

4.4 Standard of living and fertility

Retrospective fertility was analysed according to geographic area and the standard of living index (as described in Appendix 7) for certain age groups, using the indicator average number of children per woman.

The results, given in table 34, show that fertility tends to increase as standard of living decreases. Even in the age group 20-24 years, differences related to standard of living are apparent in all three regions. These differences are particularly marked in Yateras among women aged 30-59 years.

Table 34. Average number of children per woman for selected age groups according to standard of living

Standard of living and selected age groups	Plaza de la Revolución	Buenavista	Yateras
15-29 years			
Low	0.9	1.2	1.7
Medium	0.4	0.7	1.2
High	0.2	0.7	1.0
30-59 years			
Low	2.3	4.3	6.7
Medium	2.5	3.3	4.8
High	1.7	2.2	2.0
20-24 years			
Low	1.2	1.4	1.7
Medium	0.4	0.8	1.0
High	0.2	0.4	0.5
40-44 years			
Low	1.0	3.9	7.0
Medium	2.6	3.4	5.3
High	1.8	2.3	-

Source: EDEMU-82.

However, the differences between regions are still marked even when standard of living is controlled for, with fertility becoming progressively greater as one moves from the urban area of Plaza de la Revolución to the rural area of Yateras. Variations between regions are greatest among older women with low standards of living: in Plaza de la Revolución such women in the 30-59 age group have on average 2.3 children as compared to 4.3 in Buenavista and 6.7 in Yateras.

The total fertility rate serves as a basis for the analysis of current fertility - and its variations - among women with different standards of living in the study areas. The results are given in table 35. The table also shows values for the gross reproduction rate, which gives us some idea of the situation with relation to the theoretical replacement of the population according to the women's standard of living.

Through the summary indicators of present fertility obtained, the fertility behaviour in the different areas is shown in a coherent way and within each area it is broken down according to standard of living.

First, there is an increase in fertility as the area becomes more rural, and this is true for all standards of living.

Table 35. <u>Total fertility rate and gross reproduction rate according to standard of living</u>

Standard of living	Plaza de la Revolución	Buenavista	Yateras
Total fertility rate			
Low	a	1.9	3.7
Medium	1.3	1.7	2.9
High	1.0	1.4	a
All women	1.2	1.9	3.5
Gross reproduction rate			
Low	a	0.93	1.80
Medium	0.63	0.84	1.41
High	0.51	0.68	a
All women	0.59	0.93	1.71

a It was not possible to obtain a value.

Source: EDEMU-82.

Variations in fertility levels are very noticeable between Buenavista and Yateras. Taking the total of interviewed women, fertility is 94.4 per cent higher in Yateras - and there is a similar difference between the two for women with a low standard of living. For those of a medium standard of living this variation drops to 70.5 per cent. The differences in fertility levels between Plaza de la Revolución and Yateras are still more marked. At the level of the areas as a whole, fertility is 191.7 per cent higher in Yateras, and it is 123 per cent higher for women with a medium standard of living, this being the only level at which it was possible to make a separate estimate.

Second, there is a drop in fertility within each area as the standard of living increases. For Plaza de la Revolución the drop between the medium and high standards of living, for which it was possible to make an estimate, is 23.1 per cent. In Buenavista, there is a drop of 10.5 per cent between the low and medium standards of living, and 17.6 per cent between the medium and high. In Yateras, the decrease in fertility between women of the low and medium standards of living was 21.6 per cent.

Notes

[1] For readers unfamiliar with demography, definitions of these fertility measures are provided here.
Total fertility rate (TFR) for a given year indicates the average number of <u>children</u> that a woman would bear if she went

through the reproductive ages (usually assumed to be 15-49) with the age-specific fertility rates observed in the given year. In order for a population to replace itself, a total fertility rate of somewhat more than 2 is required (depending on mortality conditions).

The gross reproduction rate (GRR) in a given year is the average number of _daughters_ a woman would bear if she experienced the age-specific fertility rates observed in a given year; GRR is approximately half of TFR, being TFR divided by 1 plus the male-female sex ratio at birth.

The general fertility rate is the number of live births per thousand women aged 15 to 49 in a given year.

The crude birth rate (CBR) is the number of live births per thousand persons in the total population in a given year.

[2] The estimation of fertility levels in the three areas has been hindered by the low frequency of births in some age groups. Thus, as was explained when describing the general fertility levels, it has been necessary to make some demographic adjustments to the original data. In this way it was possible to obtain, despite the low frequency of births in the previous year, information which shows present fertility levels and which are valid for comparison.

[3] See, for example, PECFAL survey (Miro, 1968) and World Fertility Survey 1981.

[4] Alvarez and Ruben (1973), table 11, p. 24, and Alvarez, n.d., table 33, p. 52. These surveys used the concept "remunerated worker" to identify working and not working women, which leads to figures not strictly comparable with those obtained in EDEMU-82.

[5] Reservations can be made with respect to these estimates. On the fringe of the typical error of sampling, the low fertility level found in the three areas, especially among those over 35 years old, greatly reduced the number of children born the previous year and limited the value of the estimates. This reservation is valid for the total fertility of each of the areas, but even more so if women are separated according to their labour situation. However, as has been explained, the estimates and adjustments were made following methods proven in other countries (see Brass, 1974). They were applied in a similar way to working and non-working women in each area, thus making the results comparable.

CHAPTER V

IDEAL FAMILY SIZE AND SPACING OF BIRTHS

5.1 Ideal family size

In order to broaden the horizon of knowledge concerning the reproductive behaviour of women, it is useful to undertake a study of their fertility ideals, that is, to ascertain the number of children they wanted, and compare this with actual family size, as in table 36.

Table 36. Percentage distribution of women according to ideal and actual family size

Number of children	Plaza de la Revolución		Buenavista		Yateras	
	Ideal	Actual	Ideal	Actual	Ideal	Actual
None	0.2	36.8	0.1	27.7	–	19.2
One	2.2	20.1	0.9	19.5	0.3	18.1
Two	62.8	23.0	50.2	20.2	22.9	17.1
Three	28.5	10.3	38.0	13.2	32.2	12.3
Four and more	5.5	9.9	10.8	19.5	43.8	33.3
Any	0.8	n.a.	–	n.a.	0.8	n.a.
Total	100.0	100.0	100.0	100.0	100.0	100.0

n.a. = Not applicable. – = value nil or negligible.

Source: EDEMU-82.

It can be noted that while in Yateras, one out of every five women did not as yet have any children, in Plaza de la Revolución that proportion is as high as one out of three. However, virtually no woman said their ideal was to have no children.

The majority of the women in Plaza de la Revolución (approximately two out of three) and in Buenavista (one out of two) declared it as their ideal to have two children; but only 23 per cent of women in Yateras wanted to have two children or less.

The differences between the areas of low and high fertility

become even more obvious when one looks at the proportions of women whose ideal is four or more children: 5 per cent in Plaza de la Revolución, 11 per cent in Buenavista and 44 per cent in Yateras.

Thus, women have actually had fewer children than their declared ideals. This may be because the younger women have not yet completed their child-bearing. Yet in Plaza de la Revolución, for example, with a total fertility rate of 1.2, it is surprising that so few women want one child and that one in five wants three or more.

5.2 Factors related to ideal family size

The effect of educational level on ideal family size can be seen in table 37. To simplify the analysis, the average ideal number of children that women wished to have at each educational level was computed and compared with the estimations made about the actual number of children women would have at the end of their reproductive life (total fertility rate). As we know, this indicator of present fertility levels shows the potential number of children women will actually have during their lives.

Table 37. Median ideal number of children and total fertility rate according to educational level

Area and indicators	Educational level			
	Primary	Basic medium	Higher medium	Higher
Plaza de la Revolución				
Median ideal number of children	2	2	2	2
Total fertility rate	2.8	1.1	1.0	a
Buenavista				
Median ideal number of children	3	2	2	2
Total fertility rate	3.4	2.3	1.6	a
Yateras				
Median ideal number of children	4	3	3	a
Total fertility rate	3.9	3.0	a	a

a   Non-representative information.

Source: EDEMU-82.

With regard to the ideals, the table shows a rising trend from the most urban towards the most rural level. It should be

60

noted, however, that in spite of the fact that Yateras presents the highest ideals, these values are relatively low compared to many developing countries. The primary educational level has higher reproductive aspirations than the other levels in Buenavista and Yateras but not in Plaza de la Revolución. According to the results, a woman with a primary educational level in Plaza de la Revolución wants only two children compared to three for similar women in Buenavista and four in Yateras. This confirms the general trend in Plaza de la Revolución towards lower fertility ideals which are reflected in its lower fertility rate.

When comparing the ideal number of children that women said they wanted with the actual fertility rate, the figures are quite similar except in Plaza de la Revolución, where women with primary education have more than their ideal of two and those with basic medium and higher medium have less than their ideal, which is also two. Although this could suggest a potential trend towards an increase in fertility so as to bring actual family size closer to the ideal, the authors do not consider this likely.

Family size ideals are shown in table 38 according to whether women are working or not working and by occupational group for those who are working.

In Plaza de la Revolución an "ideal" of two children thus prevails independently of the labour situation and occupational category of women, as between 60 and 65 per cent of women declared that they would consider this the ideal number of children.

In the semi-urban area of Buenavista, the ideal is three children among those who do not work and women with Group III occupations, a finding which can be linked to the higher family size ideals noted earlier in the lowest educational group.

In Yateras, where between 40 and 45 per cent of women declare an ideal of more than three children, the average shows an ideal of three without differences according to labour situation or occupational groups.

These family size ideals are undoubtedly low compared with other developing countries. In addition, everything seems to indicate that the urban pattern is spreading into even the most rural areas as educational levels rise, which will lead in the future to fertility levels still lower than those experienced now.

Apart from the non-working women in Yateras, the current fertility of Cuban women is quite close to family size ideals, and in fact less than the ideal for certain groups of women in urban and semi-urban areas where other factors must be operating to result in such a low total fertility rate.

Table 38. Percentage distribution of women's ideal number of children by labour situation and occupational group

Area and labour situation	Total[a]	Ideal number of children				Median ideal	Total fertility rate
		Less than two	Two	Three	More than three		
Plaza de la Revolución							
Not working	98.8	2.8	64.6	24.9	6.5	2	1.63
Working	99.3	2.1	61.6	30.7	4.9	2	1.06
Group I	99.3	2.8	62.6	30.9	3.0	2	1.3
Group II	99.2	1.7	60.1	29.9	7.5	2	2.0
Group III	100.0	1.2	63.4	30.5	4.9	2	2.2
Buenavista							
Not working	99.5	0.7	48.4	39.6	10.8	3	2.13
Working	99.7	1.4	52.0	35.8	10.5	2	1.69
Group I	99.3	2.0	56.1	36.5	4.7	2	1.4
Group II	100.0	0.6	51.7	31.8	15.9	2	2.6
Group III	100.0	1.7	47.5	44.0	6.8	3	2.8
Yateras							
Not working	99.1	0.6	22.8	30.0	45.7	3	4.14
Working	99.2	0.0	22.8	35.4	41.0	3	2.69
Group I	100.0	0.0	34.1	31.8	34.1	3	1.5
Group II	100.0	0.0	19.4	39.4	41.2	3	3.2
Group III	97.2	0.0	18.5	32.7	46.0	3	5.2

[a] Totals do not always add up to 100 because some "did not know" or did not answer.

Source: EDEMU-82.

5.3 Birth spacing

Closely related to ideals concerning the number of children are those relating to the time between marrying and having the first child and the time between the birth of one child and the next one. In the survey women were asked about their ideals for these intervals, and the intervals they had actually experienced (table 39).

In case of the interval between marriage and the first birth, the results show an inverse relation to fertility, women with lower fertility declaring longer ideal and actual intervals.

However, women in fact waited less time than their ideal to have their first child, probably because they did not often use contraceptives during this interval, as will be discussed later. The ideal interval was about six months longer than the actual.

Table 39. Mean ideal and actual birth intervals according to age group (in years)

Interval and area	All women	15-19	20-24	25-29	0-59
Ideal interval to first birth					
Plaza de la Revolución	2.32	2.06	2.42	2.36	2.36
Buenavista	2.02	1.93	1.97	2.10	2.07
Yateras	1.77	1.67	1.74	1.72	1.88
Ideal interval between births					
Plaza de la Revolución	2.31	2.14	2.14	2.28	2.37
Buenavista	2.70	2.56	2.65	2.73	2.75
Yateras	2.93	2.90	2.98	3.13	2.87
Actual interval to first birth					
Plaza de la Revolución	1.72	1.37	1.45	1.69	1.74
Buenavista	1.44	0.91	1.49	1.35	1.51
Yateras	1.24	0.97	1.29	1.16	1.31
Actual interval between births					
Plaza de la Revolución	2.51	a	1.92	2.51	2.54
Buenavista	1.94	1.50	2.29	2.31	1.92
Yateras	1.80	a	1.89	1.77	1.81

a   Little representative value.

Source: EDEMU-82.

Unlike the interval to the first birth, the ideal interval between the first and second births presents increasing values in the more rural areas. In Plaza de la Revolución, the ideal gap of 2.3 years between children was somewhat less than the actual gap of 2.5 years. In Buenavista and Yateras, however, the ideal was greater (2.7 and 2.9 years), while the actual gap was considerably less (1.9 and 1.8 years).

The actual intervals between marriage and the first child and between the first and second child both decline as one goes from the urban area to the semi-urban area to the rural area, which corresponds with the higher fertility rates in less urbanised areas. It is also in line with the early fertility peak which is particularly marked in Yateras and Buenavista (figure 3). A particularly short interval between marriage and first birth (about 11 months) is noticeable for married women aged 15 to 19 in Buenavista and Yateras.

It is important to note that a relatively high proportion of married women were mothers before the end of their first year of marriage: about 25 per cent in Plaza de la Revolución, 30 per cent in Buenavista and 40 per cent in Yateras. Thus, it could be inferred that in many cases it was the conception that precipitated the union.

The fact that the ideal gap between marriage and the first child was greatest in Plaza de la Revolución may be partly related to the higher educational levels in the urban area, as can be seen in table 40. In both Plaza de la Revolución and Buenavista the ideal gap is greater among women with higher educational levels. However, the actual gap shows little relation to educational level. In Yateras, little variation is found among the different educational levels in either the ideal or the actual interval.

In the survey there was also a question related to the reasons why women favoured a particular interval between marriage and the first birth (question 21). In all three areas over 70 per cent of women gave as their answer either "to give time for the couple to get to know each other better" or "to enjoy the first years of married life" (EDEMU-82, table 244). This indicates a generally responsible attitude towards having a baby, in that this should only take place when there already exists a certain degree of identification between the couple.

Amongst women at the higher educational levels, the answer "to give time for the couple to get to know each other better" was more prevalent, which would indicate that the degree of responsibility increases with the educational level of the women. This conclusion is valid for all three areas surveyed. It is interesting to see that few women gave the answer "in order to work and study": as far as having a child is concerned, the stability of the couple is clearly more of an issue than any potential personal effect on the women's ability to work or study. In other words, having a child does not seem to be perceived by women as a serious obstacle to their being able to work or study.

Table 40. <u>Mean ideal and actual intervals to first birth according to educational level (in years)</u>

Area and interval	Educational level			
	Primary	Basic medium	Higher medium	University
Plaza de la Revolución				
Ideal interval	2.25	2.21	2.34	2.52
Actual interval	1.66	1.69	1.82	1.70
Buenavista				
Ideal interval	2.02	1.95	2.12	2.34
Actual interval	1.44	1.39	1.52	1.43
Yateras				
Ideal interval	1.82	1.69	1.70	[a]
Actual interval	1.27	1.19	1.19	[a]

[a] Information not representative.

Source: EDEMU-82.

When the ideal and actual gaps between marriage and first birth are analysed according to standard of living, the results are somewhat similar to those for education, since education forms part of this index (table 41). In Yateras, there is little variation in either the ideal or the actual gap, whereas in Plaza de la Revolución and Buenavista the ideal interval is longer among women with higher standards of living. In Plaza de la Revolución, however, standard of living, unlike education, is related to the actual interval, which is noticeably shorter amongst women with the lowest standard of living - in fact very similar to that found in Yateras.

As regards the ideal and actual intervals between births, averages according to educational level are shown for each region in table 42. The ideal interval between children tends to increase as one moves from the urban to the rural area; it also shows some tendency to be longer among women with lower educational levels.

Table 41. Mean ideal and actual intervals to first birth according to standard of living (in years)

Interval and standard of living	Plaza de la Revolución	Buenavista	Yateras
Ideal			
Low standard	2.11	1.88	1.82
Medium standard	2.77	2.02	1.73
High standard	2.42	2.32	1.75
Actual			
Low standard	1.33	1.43	1.25
Medium standard	1.71	1.43	1.26
High standard	1.75	1.52	1.17

Source: EDEMU-82.

When the actual intervals are compared, it can be seen that the opposite in fact occurs. The "more urban" women tend to have longer spaces between children than women from the more rural areas, and women with lower educational levels have shorter gaps than those with a higher educational level. Thus in Plaza de la Revolución, the actual interval between children tends to be longer than the ideal whereas in Yateras, where the ideal is higher, the actual interval is about one year less than

Table 42. Mean ideal and actual intervals between births according to educational level (in years)

Area and interval	Educational level			
	Primary	Basic medium	Higher medium	Higher
Plaza de la Revolución				
Ideal interval	2.41	2.28	2.21	2.38
Actual interval	2.35	2.61	2.70	2.75
Buenavista				
Ideal interval	2.81	2.61	2.58	2.25
Actual interval	1.92	1.91	2.75	2.25
Yateras				
Ideal interval	2.88	2.98	3.18	[a]
Actual interval	1.77	1.91	2.17	[a]

[a] Information not representative.
Source: EDEMU-82.

the ideal. These are the results one would expect, having in mind the trends in fertility which have been observed.

If it is possible in the future to bring the actual intervals between births closer to the ideals, the result of this longer spacing could turn out to be a reduction in present fertility levels.

Table 43 summarises the results obtained when analysing the ideal spacing of children according to women's work status. Whether women do or do not work for money, and what occupational group they fall into, does not seem to influence either the ideal or the actual interval to the first birth, as the slight variations which can be seen in the table do not allow us to conclude that there is any defined and clear association in any of the three areas analysed. However, when classifying working women according to occupational group, it can be seen that the actual interval between children is longest for Group I and diminishes towards Group III. This trend is followed in all three areas.

Table 43. <u>Mean ideal and actual birth intervals according to labour situation and occupational group</u> (in years)

Area and labour situation	Mean intervals to first birth		Mean intervals between births	
	Ideal	Actual	Ideal	Actual
Plaza de la Revolución				
Not working	2.25	1.73	2.24	2.71
Working	2.36	1.71	2.35	2.45
Group I	2.39	1.71	2.31	2.59
Group II	2.30	1.73	2.41	2.27
Group III	2.35	1.72	2.28	2.19
Buenavista				
Not working	1.93	1.41	2.73	1.98
Working	2.14	1.46	2.67	1.92
Group I	2.24	1.50	2.57	2.13
Group II	2.13	1.44	2.81	1.84
Group III	1.89	1.48	2.60	1.83
Yateras				
Not working	1.79	1.22	2.93	1.77
Working	1.75	1.27	2.93	1.84
Group I	1.66	1.26	2.94	2.20
Group II	1.73	1.19	3.02	1.79
Group III	1.85	1.38	2.78	1.85

Source: EDEMU-82.

CHAPTER VI

NUPTIALITY PATTERNS IN CUBA

This study has so far documented the nature of the decline
in Cuban fertility and its relationship to women's
socio-economic background and ideals relating to family size and
birth spacing.

A group of factors may be identified whose influence on
fertility is direct and immediate, and which provide a prima
facie explanation of changes in fertility. Some authors call
these factors "intermediate variables of fertility" or
"proximate determinants of fertility".[1]

The two main intermediate factors which directly influence
fertility in the Cuban context are nuptiality patterns,
including age at first conjugal union, and the use of
contraception and abortion. These two factors constitute the
subject of the present chapter and the next chapter
respectively.

These factors, and their differential characteristics in
each area, are studied according to women's educational level,
economic activity and standard of living, variables already
discussed in previous chapters. The idea is to determine how
these factors are related to the proximate determinants of
fertility and how these in turn influence fertility.[2]

6.1 Ideal and actual age at first marriage

It has already been suggested that age at first marriage or
consensual union could possibly be a factor in the rejuvenation
of fertility in the areas of study, i.e. the tendency for young
age groups to account for an increasing share of total
fertility. An early age at first marriage may influence
fertility in several ways, contributing both to the rejuvenation
of fertility and also to its increase, unless greater use is
made of methods of regulating fertility.

In all three areas, there was found to be a large
discrepancy between ideal and actual age at marriage. In Plaza
de la Revolución, while only 7.2 per cent of women felt that the
ideal age to marry was between 15 and 19 years old, 44.8 per
cent of married women actually did marry before the age of 20.
A similar situation was found both in Buenavista (15.8 against
63.6 per cent) and in Yateras (29.5 against 74.6 per cent).

From the above data it can be inferred that as one moves from the urban to the rural zones, the proportion of women who believe they should marry early increases and a much higher proportion actually do so.

This was also confirmed when calculating the averages for the ideal and actual ages at marriage. Although the average actual age of marriage tends to be underestimated since it is based only on women who have been married, differences in these averages across regions and over time none the less provide useful insights. In Plaza de la Revolución the ideal and actual ages were 23.2 and 20.8 years respectively; in Buenavista, 22.5 and 18.9 years, and in Yateras, 21.7 and 18.4 years.

As has been mentioned, the early age at which women have been marrying, particularly in the less urbanised areas, partly explains the increase in the relative weight of fertility of women under 20 years of age. As a result the sex education programmes, which are disseminated through the press, stress the need to avoid early marriage, explaining the physical, psychological and social repercussions that marriage at an early age may have.

Interviewees were also asked why they favoured a particular age for marriage (question 18 of questionnaire C-2). In all three areas the reason most commonly given was "because by that age women will be mature and responsible". In general, educational level did not influence this answer.

The second most important reason was "because they will have finished their studies". In Buenavista and Yateras a significant number of women answered "because they should be young and strong to raise their children". This answer was given mainly by women with primary and medium educational levels.

From the above it may be concluded that opinions as to when women mature and finish their studies vary to some extent between urban and rural areas. In the latter it is believed that women tend to mature and finish their studies a little earlier than in the urban area. These underlying conceptions go some way towards explaining the earlier age of marriage in these areas.

Finally, it is interesting to note that the reason "to avoid women having sexual relations with their boyfriends" was not mentioned by any woman in Plaza de la Revolución, only one in Buenavista, and seven at the primary and medium educational levels in Yateras. From this it can be inferred that the interviewees regarded this as a very minor consideration.

Table 44 shows the ages women considered most appropriate

for marriage according to area, labour situation and occupational group. To obtain a summary indicator the mean ideal age was estimated. The results show that there is not a significant difference as regards ideal age of marriage between those who are working and those who are not within any of the study areas. The differences between the three study areas, as noted above, are, however, evident in this table.

When the ideal age of marriage of working women is analysed according to occupational category, some differences do become apparent. In the most urban zone (Plaza de la Revolución) there seems to be a clear trend towards a later ideal age for women of Group I (managerial, professional and technical workers) compared with those of Group III (agricultural and non-agricultural workers), almost a year earlier in the latter group. This same trend, although less markedly, may be observed in Buenavista and Yateras also.

Table 44. Percentage distribution of women according to ideal age at marriage, labour situation and occupational group

Area, labour situation and occupational group	Ideal age at first marriage				
	Total[a]	15-19	20-24	25 or more	Mean age
Plaza de la Revolución					
Not working	100.0	8.0	68.3	23.7	23.07
Working	99.5	6.3	63.9	29.3	23.42
Groups[b] I	99.5	4.3	62.7	32.5	23.64
II	99.8	7.5	65.2	27.1	23.26
III	100.0	11.0	67.0	22.0	22.91
Buenavista					
Not working	100.0	16.0	66.7	17.3	22.55
Working	100.0	15.4	67.4	17.2	22.57
Groups[b] I	100.0	10.8	70.3	18.9	22.79
II	100.0	13.6	71.0	15.4	22.56
III	100.0	30.5	49.2	20.3	21.98
Yateras					
Not working	99.9	28.9	60.6	10.4	21.74
Working	99.7	30.2	58.8	10.7	21.68
Groups[b] I	100.0	18.8	64.7	16.5	22.41
II	99.4	33.3	55.8	10.3	21.50
III	100.0	34.5	59.3	6.2	21.30

[a] Totals do not always add up to 100 because some women answered "don't know" or did not answer.
[b] Group I: managerial, professional and technical workers.
    Group II: administrative and service workers.
    Group III: agricultural and non-agricultural workers.
Source: EDEMU-82.

Table 45 presents ever-married women's actual age at first marriage according to their current labour situation for each of the study areas. It can also be seen that the actual age at marriage shows greater variation between regions than does the ideal, about which there appears to be a certain consensus on the early twenties.

The group for whom the actual age of marriage is highest is working women in Plaza de la Revolución. In all other groups, the mean age of marriage is less than 20. It would thus appear that other factors besides ideas about the ideal age are having the effect of lowering the age at first conjugal union, and that these factors carry different weights in the different areas.

Table 45. Percentage distribution of ever-married women according to actual age at first marriage and labour situation

| Area and labour situation | Actual age at first marriage | | | | Mean age |
	Total[a]	15-19	20-24	25 or more	
Plaza de la Revolución					
Working	99.5	40.9	32.8	25.8	21.37
Not working	99.6	54.5	28.1	17.0	19.59
Buenavista					
Working	100.0	59.1	29.1	11.8	19.23
Not working	100.0	68.2	22.0	9.8	18.67
Yateras					
Working	100.0	71.7	23.1	5.2	18.49
Not working	100.0	76.7	20.5	2.8	18.26

[a] Totals do not always add up to 100 because some women did not answer.

Source: EDEMU-82.

As regards the differential in actual marriage age between working and non-working women, in all three areas working women tend to have contracted their first stable conjugal union at a later age than those who do not work. However, as can be seen, the difference decreases as one moves from the most urban (1.78 years) to the semi-urban (0.56 years) to the rural area (0.23 years).

One explanation may be the different occupational structure

of working women in the three areas researched. In Plaza de la Revolución working women are more likely to be in occupations which require higher qualifications calling for a higher educational level. To achieve this means a delay before the first stable conjugal union takes place. This does not happen so much in the semi-urban area, and even less so in the rural area, where women's occupations are usually more compatible with an earlier conjugal tie.

This explanation is reinforced by the figures concerning age at first conjugal union and age at first job for women who are working, as shown in table 46.

Table 46. Mean age of working women at first conjugal union and at first job, by area (in years)

Area	At first conjugal union	At first job
Plaza de la Revolución	21.37	20.88
Buenavista	19.23	20.68
Yateras	18.49	19.67

Source: EDEMU-82.

In Plaza de la Revolución, the first conjugal union tends to take place at an older age than the first job. In Buenavista and Yateras the opposite is true: the conjugal union comes first and then the job. It should also be underlined that getting the first job takes place at a significantly older age in the urban area than in the rural area. This seems to confirm that the type of occupation women tend to have in Plaza de la Revolución not only delays the age of the first conjugal union, but also that of the first job, because of the time required to obtain the necessary qualifications. The contrary is true in the analysis of the semi-urban and above all the rural areas.

We have thus seen that women tend to enter into their first stable conjugal union at an early age, particularly in the semi-urban and rural areas. There is a clear difference between working women and non-working women, with an older age among those who work, especially in the urban and semi-urban areas. The analysis by occupational group, although incomplete, also shows a trend towards an older age at first marriage for those in occupations which need more qualifications.

The labour situation and occupational group of women thus exert a significant influence on one of the most important elements of nuptiality patterns, that is, age at the first conjugal union. This influence may partly explain the differences in fertility between working and non-working women and between occupational groups.

It should also be noted that the average age at which women enter their first stable conjugal union is very low, both for working women and for non-working women. According to the experience of other countries, one would expect this to result in higher fertility levels than those found in the three areas studied.

Another factor which can be related to the ideal age of marriage is the standard of living of the women. As mentioned earlier, a standard of living index was computed, as described in Appendix 7; its relation to ideal age of marriage is shown in table 47.

Table 47. <u>Percentage distribution of women according to standard of living and ideal age at marriage</u>

Standard of living and ideal age at marriage	Plaza de la Revolución	Buenavista	Yateras
Low standard of living			
15-19	14.0	23.4	36.2
20-24	60.0	56.9	54.0
25-29	20.0	15.3	9.1
30 and over	6.0	4.4	0.7
Medium standard of living			
15-19	9.3	14.4	25.4
20-24	66.5	69.3	64.0
25-29	21.5	14.3	10.3
30 and over	2.7	2.0	0.1
High standard of living			
15-19	3.1	13.3	17.0
20-24	66.0	67.2	50.0
25-29	29.0	19.5	33.0
30 and over	1.9	-	-

Source: EDEMU-82.

The results show how, irrespective of standard of living and area of residence, at least one out of every two women said that the ideal age for a first marriage was from 20 to 24 years.

The preference for early marriage at 15-19 years of age increases as the level of socio-economic development decreases, independently of standard of living. Amongst women with a low standard of living, two and a half times as many expressed a preference for very early marriage in Yateras as compared to Plaza de la Revolución, but amongst those with a high standard of living there were more than five times as many in Yateras who favoured these ages. In all three areas, the tendency to suggest an ideal age of 15-19 is greatest at the lowest standard of living.

The inclination towards this age range could be explained by the fact that at the age of 18 the process of incorporation into economic activity has just begun - a fact which goes hand in hand with economic independence. This age also marks the conclusion of medium-level studies, both those of a technical and those of a general nature, and the beginning of university studies.

Another indicator which is relevant to this analysis is the average ideal age for marriage or consensual union. In this case the very wide differences between women in the three areas are greatly reduced.

Thus, the average ideal age of women in Yateras with a low standard of living is a little under two years lower than similar women from Plaza de la Revolución; for those with a medium standard of living the difference is one year and for those with a high standard of living there is hardly any difference. The results reached are given in table 48.

Table 48. Average ideal age at marriage according to standard of living (in years)

Standard of living	Plaza de la Revolución	Buenavista	Yateras
Low	23.0	22.3	21.3
Medium	23.1	22.6	21.9
High	23.5	22.7	23.3
All women	23.2	22.5	21.7

Source: EDEMU-82.

6.2 Conjugal situation

The study of variations in marriage rates, and the repercussions for fertility, also provide some interesting results. If the married women and those in a consensual union are grouped together, calling them all women in a conjugal union, we find that in Plaza de la Revolución 54.1 per cent of women are in a conjugal union, in Buenavista 69.4 per cent and in Yateras 73.9 per cent. This is directly proportional to the fertility levels of the three areas: a lower proportion of women in a conjugal union corresponds to a lower fertility level.

An analysis of marital status by age group (table 49) helps explain the differences in fertility between the areas. Thus, the degree of rejuvenation of fertility is strongly correlated with the proportion of women under 30 years of age in a conjugal union. The greater rejuvenation of fertility in Yateras can be explained by the fact that it has the highest proportion of women under 30 in a conjugal union: 68.3 per cent. At the other extreme is Plaza de la Revolución, with both a lesser degree of rejuvenation and a lower proportion of women under 30 in a conjugal union: 33.6 per cent. While in Plaza de la Revolución well over half the women from 15 to 29 years old were still single, in Yateras only one in five was still single.

Table 49. <u>Percentage distribution of women according to marital status and age group</u>

Marital status		Age group		
	Total	15-29	30-49	50-59
		Plaza de la Revolución		
Total	100.0	100.0	100.0	100.0
Married	46.2	26.5	59.2	55.2
Consensual union	7.9	7.1	9.5	5.3
Widowed	2.9	0	1.6	12.5
Separated	19.4	9.9	26.8	21.0
Single	23.6	56.5	2.9	6.0
		Buenavista		
Total	100.0	100.0	100.0	100.0
Married	53.1	37.5	67.8	64.5
Consensual union	16.3	17.6	15.2	16.1
Widowed	2.5	0.2	1.8	14.0
Separated	10.7	10.1	12.8	5.4
Single	17.4	34.6	2.4	0
		Yateras		
Total	100.0	100.0	100.0	100.0
Married	21.8	16.8	30.2	20.1
Consensual union	52.1	51.5	54.7	46.3
Widowed	2.0	0.2	2.6	11.6
Separated	12.4	11.8	10.9	22.0
Single	11.7	19.7	1.6	0

Source: EDEMU-82.

Another aspect worth examining is the proportion of women under 30 in a consensual union. In Latin America generally the fertility rate tends to be higher amongst women with this marital status. The results of this survey provide further confirmation of this tendency: in Plaza de la Revolución, the area with the lowest fertility, the percentage of all women in a conjugal situation who are in a consensual union is 15 per cent, whereas it is 23 per cent in Buenavista and 71 per cent in Yateras.

In addition, the proportion of separated women amongst those aged 30 and over was very high in Plaza de la Revolución. For women in Yateras over 50 years of age the figure is also high: it is possible that the exodus of men working outside the municipality may have been an important factor.

When linking marital status with educational level, some interesting results are found. The most outstanding relates to the category of single women. In all three areas, most single women have a basic medium or higher medium level of education. This indicates that the younger generation will enter marriage or consensual union with a higher educational level and potentially a lower fertility level than the women who are at present in a conjugal union, the majority of whom, as we can see from table 50, have mostly a primary level.

Comparing the educational levels of women who are married with those in consensual unions, it is apparent that, in all three areas, married women tend to have higher educational levels than those in consensual unions: in Yateras, for example, 57 per cent of married women have only primary education as compared to 72 per cent of women in consensual unions.

Table 51 analyses the proportions of women married or in a consensual union according to labour situation and occupational group.

As noted earlier, the lowest proportion of women in conjugal unions is found in Plaza de la Revolución, a phenomenon linked to a later age of marriage and a higher proportion of separated women. It might be expected that the proportion in a conjugal union would be lower among working women. In Buenavista and Yateras, however, there is little difference, and in Plaza de la Revolución, there is actually a lower proportion of women in conjugal unions among non-working women – though this is related to the number of women under 25 who are single and not yet working.

When analysing the proportions of working women in a conjugal union according to occupational group, a clearer situation may be observed. This is, above all, because the age

77

Table 50. **Percentage distribution of women according to educational level and conjugal situation**

Conjugal situation and area	Educational level				
	Primary	Basic medium	Higher medium	University	Total
Married					
Plaza de la Revolución	32.5	23.2	30.2	14.1	100
Buenavista	57.7	23.6	15.7	3.0	100
Yateras	57.0	33.8	8.7	0.5	100
Consensual union					
Plaza de la Revolución	45.2	29.8	16.9	8.1	100
Buenavista	73.9	20.9	5.2	0.0	100
Yateras	71.7	23.8	4.3	0.2	100
Widowed					
Plaza de la Revolución	71.7	11.0	13.0	4.3	100
Buenavista	65.0	20.0	15.0	0.0	100
Yateras	94.4	5.6	0.0	0.0	100
Separated					
Plaza de la Revolución	32.5	22.0	30.8	14.7	100
Buenavista	56.3	27.6	13.8	2.3	100
Yateras	58.6	35.1	6.3	0.0	100
Single					
Plaza de la Revolución	8.9	43.8	41.9	5.4	100
Buenavista	14.1	63.4	19.7	2.8	100
Yateras	29.8	56.7	13.5	0.0	100

Source: EDEMU-82.

structure of occupational groups is more homogeneous both within each area and between the three areas.

The proportion of working women in a conjugal union is considerably less in Plaza de la Revolución than in the other areas. Working women in Group I occupations and also, to a lesser extent, Group II occupations, are less likely to be in a conjugal union than those in Group III occupations. These data thus help explain the lower fertility of working women in Plaza de la Revolución as compared to working women in other areas, and the variations in fertility between women in different occupational groups.

Table 51. <u>Proportion of women in a conjugal union (married or in consensual union), according to labour situation and occupational group</u>

Labour situation	Plaza de la Revolución	Buenavista	Yateras
Working	61.8	72.0	72.8
Not working	42.1	67.2	74.7
Occupational groups[a]			
I	60.5	70.3	67.1
II	61.7	71.6	73.9
III	64.6	78.0	74.3

[a]
   I Managerial, professional and technical workers.
  II Administrative and service workers.
 III Agricultural and non-agricultural workers.

Source: EDEMU-82.

6.3 <u>Number of conjugal unions</u>

In the survey women were asked how many times they had married or entered into a consensual union. In general terms it can be observed that more than 25 per cent of the women interviewed, irrespective of educational level, had been married or entered into a consensual union two or more times - a finding which, in the authors' opinion, calls for additional research.

Table 52 analyses the number of conjugal unions women said they had had, according to their labour situation and occupational group. One would expect the number of conjugal unions to be influenced by the women's age: that is, older women will be more likely to have had more than one union. This obviously has a bearing on the figures shown in the table, which should therefore be treated with some caution, especially when the comparisons refer to working and non-working women where the age structures of the categories noticeably differ.

The first thing to note is that the proportion of working women who have had more than one conjugal union is higher than for non-working women both in the most urban area and in the rural one. In the semi-urban area of Buenavista, although the opposite is true, the differences are not so significant.

This suggests a link between women's labour activity and marital instability. It also helps explain the lower fertility of working women, as they obviously have a less stable

Table 52. **Percentage distribution of women according to number of conjugal unions, labour situation and occupational group**

Area, labour situation and occupational group	Number of conjugal unions			
	Total[a]	One	Two	Three and more
Plaza de la Revolución				
Not working	100.0	76.5	17.6	5.9
Working	99.7	64.4	27.9	7.4
Group I	99.3	70.5	23.6	5.2
Group II	100.0	58.6	30.8	10.6
Group III	99.9	58.3	34.7	6.9
Buenavista				
Not working	100.0	70.7	24.1	5.2
Working	100.0	73.4	22.8	3.8
Group I	100.0	81.1	15.7	3.2
Group II	100.0	65.6	29.5	4.9
Group III	100.0	78.6	19.6	1.8
Yateras				
Not working	99.8	67.5	24.7	7.6
Working	99.4	58.0	34.0	7.4
Group I	100.0	73.1	26.9	0.0
Group II	99.3	54.7	35.3	9.3
Group III	99.0	52.4	37.9	8.7

a   Totals do not always add up to 100 because some women either said they did not know or did not answer.

Source: EDEMU-82.

reproductive life. This is most apparent in Yateras, where 41.4 per cent of working women said they had had more than one conjugal union as against 32.3 per cent among non-working women. In Plaza de la Revolución the figures are 35.3 and 23.5 per cent respectively - appreciably lower. Here one must take into account, in the case of Yateras, the labour force migration, principally male, to areas of greater employment opportunities, which must affect the conjugal situation. It is also likely that a higher proportion of separated women remarry in Yateras than in Plaza de la Revolución.

The analysis of working women according to occupational group shows that marital stability is greater among managerial, professional and technical workers - though even in this occupational category almost one quarter of women have had at least two conjugal unions. In the other two occupational groups this proportion is about one-third.

Notes

[1] See, among others, Davis and Blake (1967) and Bongaarts (1982).

[2] Obviously, the relation is not as lineal or simple as is suggested here. It would also be valid to study the relationship in the opposite direction.

CHAPTER VII

INDUCED ABORTION AND CONTRACEPTION

As has been seen, Cuban fertility has experienced a rapid fall during the last decade. Given the relatively early age of marriage or consensual union among Cuban women, the main reason for this decline cannot be found in a postponement of marriage, as is the case in certain other developing countries. The fairly high proportion of women of fertile age who are separated from their husbands may be one direct factor. Another direct determinant of this decrease is certainly the increase in the use of contraceptive methods and abortion.

There is a close interrelation between the incidence of abortion and the degree of use of contraception. In general, a greater availability of contraception will mean a reduction in the number of abortions - something for which Cuban doctors have striven, because of the harmful effects of abortion on women's health.

7.1 Abortion

Abortion has played an important role in the reduction of fertility in Cuba. Between 1968 and 1974 the rate per thousand women of reproductive age increased four times (Farnos, Gonzalez and Hernandez, 1985, p. 226). However, as can be seen in table 53, the abortion rate has been declining in recent years. The work carried out by the Sex Education Working Group, in co-ordination with the Cuban Women's Federation, in publicising the negative effects of abortion, has greatly contributed to this decline.

It is in Plaza de le Revolución, the urban zone, that the most abortions are carried out, and it is therefore the area which shows the most drastic reductions between 1971 and 1982. Except for the 30-34 age group, which shows an increase (which could be attributed to contingent error), all age groups show reductions. The most noticeable reductions are in women over 40. The higher incidence of abortion in Plaza de la Revolución may be related to the availability of health facilities and the opportunity this offers to women to make use of abortion as a means of birth control.

It will be noted that the average number of abortions among women from 15 to 19 years in Plaza de la Revolución is extremely low, with little variation between 1971 and 1982. This tallies

Table 53. <u>Average number of abortions per woman according to age group and different surveys</u>

| Age group | Plaza de la Revolución | | Buenavista | Yateras | |
	MINSAP (1971)	EDEMU (1982)	EDEMU (1982)	MINSAP (1972)	EDEMU (1982)
All women	1.06	0.77	0.57	0.36	0.21
15-19	0.07	0.06	0.07	0.05	0.04
20-24	0.39	0.25	0.52	0.18	0.12
25-29	1.02	0.91	0.78	0.30	0.36
30-34	1.05	1.10	0.87	0.52	0.27
35-39	1.33	1.21	0.76	0.60	0.33
40-44	1.71	1.11	0.67	0.64	0.27
45-49	1.97	1.19	0.82	0.79	0.18

Sources: EDEMU-82;   Alvarez and Ruben, 1973, table 5, p. 18;
Alvarez, n.d., table 14, p. 33.

with the relatively high fertility rate of this group of women, as has already been discussed. As it is almost always the first child, few women wish to avoid it or to interrupt their pregnancy. A major aim of the Sex Education Working Group's campaign has been to prevent women interrupting their first pregnancy.

Yateras, in contrast, is typical of the rural zones in having fewer abortions and one of the highest fertility rates in the country. Despite abortion levels much lower than those of Plaza de la Revolución in 1972, the decline is also apparent in Yateras. Although the sample size is relatively small, the results suggest an important reduction in the average number of abortions per women over 30 years of age in Yateras, much higher proportionately than in Plaza de la Revolución. Since those age groups are the ones that have made the greatest contribution to the reduction in fertility in Yateras, this could be indicative both of a greater maturity and of a wider knowledge and use of contraceptives to prevent pregnancies.

Finally, according to MINSAP's survey, the average number of abortions per woman is higher amongst the older age groups. It should be remembered that this indicator gathers the accumulated experiences of each group of women. If we bear in mind that the greater use of contraceptive methods (among them the intra-uterine device and the pill) began in the 1960s, it can be inferred that before then abortion occupied (as it still does) an important role as a regulator of fertility, and therefore that older women would have made more use of it. The data also indicate that since the 1960s women have had a far greater knowledge of contraceptives, using them both more widely and more efficiently.

Although all this would lead one to expect that the number of abortions per woman would increase as a function of age, the information gathered in EDEMU-82 does not reflect such an increase. The possibility that contingent errors in the data gathered, wrong declarations, and so on, might have influenced the results must therefore be stressed.

Table 54 shows the average number of abortions per woman in the 1982 survey as a function of educational level and age.

Table 54. Average number of abortions per woman for selected age groups according to educational level

Age group and educational level	Plaza de la Revolución	Buenavista	Yateras
15-19 years			
Primary	0.00	0.21	0.03
Basic medium	0.08	0.04	0.06
Higher medium	0.04	0.04	0.00
University	a	a	a
20-24 years			
Primary	0.67	0.57	0.16
Basic medium	0.27	0.54	0.13
Higher medium	0.19	0.52	0.04
University	0.24	a	a
25-29 years			
Primary	0.40	0.60	0.40
Basic medium	1.52	0.97	0.30
Higher medium	0.59	0.64	0.23
University	0.65	a	a
45-49 years			
Primary	1.47	0.89	0.16
Basic medium	1.21	0.70	a
Higher medium	0.73	a	a
University	0.80	a	a

a   Information not available or unreliable.

Source: EDEMU-82.

The first three age groups were chosen because they were considered representative of the behaviour of the most recent generations, least affected by historical factors and with the highest fertility levels. The group which was practically ending its fertile period was introduced for purposes of comparison. Because of limited data there are no figures for some categories.

If the trends for the younger age groups are analysed for each area, comparing the different educational levels, it does not seem that there is in fact much difference between the educational groups with regard to the use of abortion. This is possibly due to the wide availability of health facilities in Cuba and to the level of knowledge amongst an increasingly well-educated population.

Table 55 shows the abortion rate for women under 30 years and 30-49 years, according to the standard of living of the women. Results were also analysed for two groups of women separated in time - ages 20-24 years and 40-44 years.

Table 55. <u>Average number of abortions per woman according to standard of living and selected age groups</u>

Age group and standard of living	Plaza de la Revolución	Buenavista	Yateras
15-29 years			
Low	0.71	0.26	0.14
Medium	0.72	0.22	0.28
High	0.27	0.53	0.00
30-49 years			
Low	0.81	0.68	0.24
Medium	1.21	0.75	0.28
High	1.10	1.48	0.00
20-24 years			
Low	1.00	0.50	0.09
Medium	0.23	0.54	0.15
High	0.24	0.43	a
40-44 years			
Low	1.67	0.55	0.32
Medium	1.08	0.71	0.23
High	1.08	0.57	a

a Information unreliable due to small samples.

Source: EDEMU 1982.

The figures in table 55 highlight the following points.

The rates of abortion in the four age groups analysed do not show any systematic trends related to standard of living, although it is true that the highest rates are generally found in Plaza de la Revolución and the lowest in Yateras. The greatest variations in the average number of abortions per woman for the 15-29 age group are found in the area of Plaza de la Revolución: for women with a low standard of living the figure is 2.7 times higher than for those with a high standard. For Buenavista, the relationship is the opposite: the rate of abortion is highest for women with a high standard of living, about twice that for those with a low or medium standard.

For the 30-49 age group, too, the most outstanding differences according to standard of living are found in Plaza de la Revolución, the rates for women with a medium standard being 40 per cent higher than for those with a low standard. In Buenavista, the most significant variation is between women with low and high standards of living, the rate for the latter being 11 per cent higher.

For the two quinquennial groups analysed (20-24 years and 40-44 years), the highest incidence of abortion is found among the older women, although in the case of Buenavista the difference is not so significant. The young city women with a low standard of living have an abortion rate four times higher than those with a higher standard. For women from 40 to 44 years this figures decreases to 1.55. For Buenavista the variations both between standards of living and between age groups are much lower. In the case of Yateras the rates for those standards of living where it was possible to obtain the indicator (low and medium) were very low.

The lower fertility rates among working women as compared to non-working women in all three areas would lead one to expect a greater incidence of abortion among working women. As shown in table 56, this is in fact the case in Plaza de la Revolución and Buenavista but not in Yateras.

The tendency towards a greater use of abortion among working women is therefore also conditioned by the level of urbanisation. This constitutes a partial explanation for the lower fertility levels seen in Plaza de la Revolución and the higher fertility in Yateras.

An analysis of the incidence of abortion according to the occupations of working women shows that in the urban and semi-urban areas the average number of abortions per woman increases from those with Group I occupations through to those with Group III occupations. Thus women in Group III not only have more children than the other working women (see table 33) but also more abortions. It is possible that other factors, like the educational level required for the different occupations, which decreases from Group I to Group III, contribute to the varying incidence of abortion in different groups.

Table 56. Average number of abortions per woman from 20 to 49 years old, according to labour situation and occupational group

Area, labour situation and occupational group	Average number of abortions
Plaza de la Revolución	
Not working	0.80
Working	1.00
Group I	0.93
Group II	1.15
Group III	1.58
Buenavista	
Not working	0.67
Working	0.82
Group I	0.66
Group II	0.82
Group III	1.76
Yateras	
Not working	0.25
Working	0.26
Group I	0.16
Group II	0.20
Group III	0.17

Source: EDEMU-82.

7.2 Knowledge of contraception

Before looking at knowledge of contraceptive methods, it should be explained that the method used in putting the questions in the present survey and in MINSAP were different. In the latter the different methods were explained to the interviewee and then she was asked if she knew of them or not. In EDEMU-82 women were asked what methods they knew about but none was mentioned.

As can be seen in table 57, almost 100 per cent of women had some knowledge of contraceptive methods, the figure being slightly higher in the urban and semi-urban areas.

Table 57. Proportion of women with knowledge of various contraceptive methods according to different surveys

| Method | Plaza de la Revolución | | Buenavista | Yateras | |
	MINSAP (1971)	EDEMU (1982)	EDEMU (1982)	MINSAP (1971)	EDEMU (1982)
Intra-uterine device	98.6	94.9	91.2	94.0	97.3
Pill	40.2	92.1	86.1	7.4	72.1
Diaphragm	90.5	53.6	34.1	10.1	12.7
Condom	92.7	51.8	42.8	69.4	50.1
Female sterilisation	95.4	23.1	22.8	84.0	45.5
Rhythm method	78.2	17.0	4.0	22.7	1.6
Jellies	63.4	15.7	18.6	18.7	12.3
Coitus interruptus (withdrawal)	64.0	10.8	2.5	31.5	6.9
Vaginal washings	49.5	9.0	7.6	27.5	5.2
Male sterilisation	16.8	a	a	a	a
Vaginal suppository	49.5	a	a	17.1	a
Others	a	4.5	2.2	a	3.2
Total	b	99.5	98.9	b	98.5

a Method not investigated in the survey.
b Information not available.

Sources: EDEMU-82;   Alvarez, n.d., p. 25;   Alvarez and Ruben, 1973, p. 15.

According to both surveys, the intra-uterine device (IUD) is the contraceptive method most widely known amongst women in all three areas. It should be pointed out here that, according to the present survey, it was most widely known in Yateras. This constitutes a considerable achievement of the campaign to reduce regional disparities within the country. Apart from the different ways in which the question was formulated in the two surveys, it should also be borne in mind that changes have taken place in the preferences of women and in the availability of the different methods.

Such is certainly the case with the pill: in MINSAP's surveys in Plaza de la Revolución and Yateras it occupied only tenth place, while in EDEMU-82 it came second in all three areas, and the proportion of women who said they knew of it increased substantially. The second best-known method in MINSAP's survey in Plaza de la Revolución was "female sterilisation", but in 1982 this occupied fifth place. In Yateras, it went from second to fourth place.

According to EDEMU-82 the third best-known method in Plaza de la Revolución is the diaphragm, followed closely by the condom and then by female sterilisation. In Buenavista and Yateras, on the other hand, the condom has third place, owing perhaps to its greater availability.

It is significant that female sterilisation occupies fourth place and is better known in Yateras, possibly because of the high number of children women already had in that area.

It is interesting to compare the data obtained in the World Fertility Survey (WFS, 1980) on eight Latin American countries and ten countries of Asia and the Pacific with the information obtained in EDEMU-82. It should, however, be noted that EDEMU-82 is not, strictly speaking, completely comparable with the WFS; while the first deals with three areas of Cuba which are not representative of the country, the second involved national surveys. In the WFS only women who had been married were asked about their knowledge of contraception, while in Cuba single women were also included. Finally, in the WFS, although the various contraceptive methods were not mentioned initially when women were interviewed, they were mentioned in cases where a woman did not know of any method, so that she could answer. As has already been said, in EDEMU-82 no method was ever mentioned.

Bearing in mind these differences, it is none the less useful to make the comparison.

As the "total" column of table 58 shows, some knowledge of contraceptive methods is almost universal amongst the women of the three surveyed areas in Cuba, with a similar situation in Bangladesh, Costa Rica, the Dominican Republic, Jamaica, the Republic of Korea and Panama. Apart from Bangladesh, these countries have all experienced a reduction in fertility in recent years, and the knowledge of contraceptive methods, which is obviously a necessary condition for their use, might have been associated with this reduction.

In six of the WFS countries, as in the three areas of Cuba, the two best-known methods are precisely those of most recent introduction, the pill and the intra-uterine device. Female sterilisation is also of great importance: it is the best-known contraceptive method in three countries, with values between 78 and 95 per cent; it occupies second place in seven countries, and it is known to well over 50 per cent of women in most countries. In six countries over 50 per cent of the women interviewed had heard of male sterilisation.

In the two regions of the world shown, the best-known method is the pill, followed by the intra-uterine device, female sterilisation, the condom and male sterilisation in that order.

Table 58. Percentage of women from selected countries with knowledge of various contraceptive methods, 1974-78 and 1982[a]

Regions and countries	Pill	Intra-uterine device	Condom	Sterilisation Female	Male	Total
Asia and the Pacific (1974-78)						
Bangladesh	63.9	40.1	21.1	3.1	51.4	81.8
Fiji	98.4	96.9	83.2	95.9	39.7	99.9
Indonesia	70.8	50.0	40.7	11.3	7.9	76.8
Korea, Republic of	93.8	91.1	75.3	65.8	83.6	97.2
Malaysia	87.8	39.6	51.7	73.0		91.9
Nepal	12.0	6.0	4.8	13.0	15.7	22.4
Pakistan	63.0	48.0	14.0	7.0	2.0	75.0
Philippines	90.2	86.2	87.6	74.7	69.6	94.2
Sri Lanka	79.0	62.0	51.0	82.0	38.0	90.0
Thailand	91.7	85.5	48.0	86.8	70.0	96.4
Latin America (1974-78)						
Colombia	90.0	82.0	60.0	72.0	38.0	95.8
Costa Rica	97.9	91.5	91.0	93.8	67.2	99.5
Dominican Republic	92.4	77.6	71.6	94.8	30.3	97.5
Guyana	78.1	79.2	73.0	78.8	22.3	95.4
Jamaica	95.1	84.6	89.9	88.1	39.8	98.0
Mexico	82.6	75.2	42.2	67.6	38.1	89.5
Panama	95.2	88.7	56.0	92.9	64.9	98.6
Peru	63.3	49.4	39.6	59.5	18.9	82.0
Cuba (1982)						
Plaza de la Revolución	92.1	94.9	51.8	23.1	b	99.5
Buenavista	86.1	91.2	42.8	22.8	b	98.9
Yateras	72.1	97.3	50.1	45.5	b	98.5

a   In the 1974-78 WFS survey only women who had been married were interviewed; in the Cuban survey single women were included also.

b   Method not investigated in the research.

Sources: EDEMU-82; Concepción, 1982, Vol. I, p. 228, table 15.

In the three areas studied in Cuba, the two most widely known methods are the intra-uterine device and the pill, and to a lesser extent the condom.

7.3 Use of contraception

Table 59 shows the proportions of women who said they had used some contraceptive methods at some time. Again, the different ways in which the questions were asked in the MINSAP and EDEMU-82 surveys should be taken into account.

Table 59. Percentage of women from 15 to 49 years who have ever used any contraceptive method

Method	Plaza de la Revolución		Buenavista	Yateras	
	MINSAP (1971)	EDEMU (1982)	EDEMU (1982)	MINSAP (1972)	EDEMU (1982)
Intra-uterine device	28.5	43.7	44.6	28.6	60.8
Pill	2.8	24.6	15.6	b	7.3
Diaphragm	9.5	8.7	2.1	b	0.5
Condom	31.6	7.1	9.3	12.5	4.1
Female sterilisation	7.4	9.7	17.7	5.1	14.2
Rhythm or calendar	25.7	4.7	1.9	6.1	0.1
Jellies	12.6	2.3	2.4	3.5	1.5
Coitus interruptus (withdrawal)	25.0	1.7	1.1	13.4	1.5
Vaginal washings	24.5	1.2	2.0	3.8	0.5
Vaginal suppository	9.6	a	a	2.1	a
Total	b	66.2	66.8	b	74.2

a Method not investigated in the survey.
b Information not available.

Sources: Alvarez, 1982; EDEMU-82.

The first conclusion is that the proportion of women who had ever used some method of contraception in 1982 is high - about two-thirds in Plaza de la Revolución and Buenavista and 74 per cent in Yateras. The higher value in Yateras, the rural area, may be related to the lower proportion of single women in this area. It can also be linked to a much lower use of abortion, and to the efforts made by the health authorities to reduce the incidence of abortion, substituting for it a greater knowledge of contraceptive methods.

The figures obtained in the MINSAP survey do not permit a direct comparison of the total proportions of women who have ever used contraception. Nevertheless, it is clear that there has been a spectacular increase in the use of the IUD, particularly in Yateras where 60.8 per cent of the women had used an IUD in 1982 compared with only 28.6 per cent ten years earlier. Another method showing an increase is female sterilisation, particularly in Yateras, where 14 per cent of the women interviewed had been sterilised, and in Buenavista, where about 18 per cent had been sterilised. In Plaza de la Revolución, there has been an enormous increase in the proportion who have used the pill, this proportion being somewhat greater than in Buenavista and much greater than in Yateras. Also in Plaza de la Revolución, there has been little change in users of the diaphragm which is hardly used in the other areas. The methods which have been decreasing in popularity are the condom, rhythm method, jellies, vaginal washings and coitus interruptus - all less reliable methods than those with increasing popularity. This switch to more reliable methods which require medical services testifies to the wide availability of such services, even in a rural area such as Yateras. It has also no doubt contributed to the decline in abortions as well as the decline in fertility.

When comparing the data from Cuba with the WFS survey previously mentioned (table 60), it is noticeable that the proportions of women who have used contraception in the three Cuban areas are similar to those of three other countries - Fiji, Panama and Jamaica - which have also experienced a marked decline in fertility. Only Costa Rica, which has experienced a moderate decline in fertility in recent years, shows a substantially higher percentage of contraceptive users.

If single women are excluded to make the data directly comparable for Cuba, then the values for all three areas are higher than those for any other country. In Plaza de la Revolución 84.3 per cent of women from 15 to 49 years who have ever been married have used some form of contraception, while the values for Buenavista and Yateras are 85.1 and 84.8 per cent respectively.

In 14 of the 17 WFS countries the pill was the method most widely used; although there is a large variation in the actual percentage between countries, only Costa Rica exceeds 50 per cent. In a number of these countries, the rhythm method and coitus interruptus (the withdrawal method) are relatively widely used. In the three areas considered in EDEMU-82, as has been seen, the IUD is the most widely used method, far surpassing use in any other country, and widely surpassing the second method, which in Plaza de la Revolución is the pill and in Buenavista and Yateras, female sterilisation.

93

Table 60. Percentage of women from selected countries who have ever used any contraceptive method, 1974-78[a] and 1982

Regions and countries	Pill	Intra-uterine device	Condom	Sterilisation Female	Sterilisation Male	Rhythm	Coitus interruptus (withdrawal)	Total
Asia and the Pacific (1974-78)								
Bangladesh	5.0	0.9	4.8	0.3	0.4	4.5	2.6	13.6
Fiji	30.5	16.1	16.1	15.3	-	15.5	15.2	67.6
Indonesia	-	-	-	-	-	-	-	34.4
Korea, Republic of	33.4	24.9	21.5	1.7	3.1	16.1	11.8	56.6
Malaysia	31.5	1.5	8.5	3.3	0.3	10.3	7.7	47.6
Nepal	1.7	0.2	0.6	0.1	1.4	0	0	4.1
Pakistan	4.0	4.0	3	1.0				10.0
Philippines	24.7	7.0	20.1	4.5	0.6	23.1	31.0	57.5
Sri Lanka	8.0	8.0	5.0	8.0	1.0	22.0	6.0	43.2
Thailand	25.7	9.3	3.5	6.0	1.9	15.4[c]		45.2
Latin America (1974-78)								
Colombia	33.0	15.0	8.0	4.0	0.0	18.0	17.0	59.0
Costa Rica	50.6	12.3	35.5	12.1	0.9	20.2	25.4	81.6
Dominican Republic	19.7	6.7	10.5	10.9	0.0	7.0	18.6	47.3
Guyana	20.7	8.2	16.6	8.1	0.0	11.0	14.0	57.5
Jamaica	32.8	8.3	27.1	8.0	0.0	4.8	20.1	65.9
Mexico	25.7	8.1	6.6	2.7	0.2	12.8	17.6	45.2
Panama	42.1	8.4	12.9	20.5	0.3	15.5	17.9	72.6
Peru	13.4	2.5	6.8	2.6	-	26.6	16.5	48.5
Cuba (1982)								
Plaza de la Revolución	24.6	43.7	7.1	9.7	b	4.7	1.7	66.2
Buenavista	16.6	44.6	9.3	17.7	b	1.9	1.1	66.8
Yateras	7.3	60.8	4.1	14.2	b	0.1	1.5	74.2

a In the 1974-78 WFS survey only women who had been married were interviewed.
b Method not researched in the survey.
c Also includes abstinence.

Sources: EDEMU-82; Concepción, 1982, Vol. I, p. 228, table 15.

The data on current use of contraception presented in table 61 also indicate that one cause of the impressive recent decline in fertility in the areas studied must be an increase in the use of contraception combined with a switch to more reliable methods. Comparing the MINSAP surveys with EDEMU-82, Plaza de la Revolución presents notable increases in the proportion of women using the IUD and sterilisation. In Yateras, the use of both these contraceptive methods has increased even more spectacularly.

Table 61. <u>Percentage distribution of women currently using some form of contraception, according to different surveys</u>

Method	Plaza de la Revolución		Buenavista	Yateras	
	MINSAP (1971)	EDEMU (1982)	EDEMU (1971)	MINSAP (1972)	EDEMU (1982)
Intra-uterine device	17.3	22.7	27.8	16.5	39.6
Pill	a	8.3	6.3	a	4.1
Diaphragm	a	1.2	0	a	0
Condom	7.0	2.9	1.4	3.5	0.2
Female sterilisation	7.3	9.7	18.3	5.1	14.3
Rhythm or calendar	8.0	2.2	0.9	3.1	0
Jellies	a	0.1	0.1	a	0.2
Withdrawal	7.5	0.4	0.4	6.4	0.4
Vaginal washing	7.7	0.2	0	a	0
Others	a	0.3	0.1	a	0.4
Total	a	45.9	55.2	a	58.9

a Information not available or not representative.

Sources: Alvarez and Ruben, 1973, p. 17; Alvarez, n.d., p. 29; EDEMU-82.

The contraceptive pill, which requires a certain degree of education for its use, also shows consistent values between the areas. In effect, the proportion of women who use it in Plaza de la Revolución is twice that of Yateras. The relatively low values reported for this method are explained by its relatively recent introduction into the country - although it is already one of the main contraceptive methods used by women in the study areas.

It could well be that the lower proportion of contraceptive users in Plaza de la Revolución may be related to the proportion of women not in a conjugal union (single women, widows and divorcees). In fact, if all women are considered irrespective of marital status, the percentages of women who use contraceptives are 45.9 for Plaza de la Revolución, 55.2 for Buenavista and 58.9 for Yateras; if only married women and women in a consensual union are considered, however, the respective proportions increase to 67.1, 73.7 and 69.8 per cent respectively, almost eliminating the differences between the areas.

There is also a clear relationship between the use of abortion and contraception: the areas which reported a higher use of abortion present a lower use of contraception and vice versa.

The data presented in table 62 also reflect a coherent pattern of behaviour. In all three areas the proportion of women using contraception increases as they have more children.

With respect to differences between areas, the proportion using contraception is greater in areas of higher fertility among women with two or more children; this explains, in part, why women in the areas where fertility was high some years ago have contributed the most to the recent decline in fertility. On the other hand, among women with no children, one out of five uses contraception in Plaza de la Revolución, while in Buenavista and Yateras the proportion is only one out of ten.

Table 62. Percentage of women currently using contraception according to number of children born alive

Number of children	Plaza de la Revolución	Buenavista	Yateras
All women	45.9	55.2	58.9
None	20.8	9.9	8.6
One	59.6	65.4	60.9
Two	64.6	78.4	78.9
Three	69.3	78.7	79.8
Four and more	56.5	81.7	73.4

Source: EDEMU-82.

The high proportion of women in Yateras who use contraception should be underlined. The province where Yateras is located used to be part of the old province of Oriente, which had the highest fertility levels of the country. The figures for contraceptive use corroborate the marked process of homogenisation that is taking place in Cuba, in that every couple, in every part of the country, is guaranteed access to the means to control their fertility, as well as the necessary education and information, to enable them to have the number of children they wish.

Similarly, the figures of current contraceptive use by age as shown in table 63 confirm the very high percentage of users in all areas, particularly after age 25. These percentages are particularly high given the proportion of women not in a conjugal union (see table 49).

Table 63. <u>Proportion of women who currently use contraception according to age group</u>

Age group	Plaza de la Revolución	Buenavista	Yateras
All women	45.9	55.2	58.9
15-19	9.2	15.0	27.6
20-24	47.2	50.4	56.5
25-29	72.0	67.6	73.7
30-34	62.2	79.2	70.3
35-39	63.4	77.0	75.8
40-44	53.5	70.0	76.4
45-49	40.2	62.8	48.0

Source: EDEMU-82.

Table 64 presents WFS data on contraceptive use from selected developing countries according to age, number of living children and place of residence in 1974-78, alongside the EDEMU-82 data. As pointed out in notes (a) and (e), although the WFS data are not strictly comparable with that on the three areas of Cuba, they do at least allow us to place these areas, in a general way, within the context of the 18 countries included in the table.

Taking the 15-24 age group, the proportion of contraceptive users in Plaza de la Revolución is lower than that found in all but five of the WFS countries, while only four countries have a higher proportion than Yateras. The higher (lower) proportion of ever-married women in this age group in Yateras (Plaza de la Revolución) may partly explain this difference.

In every country surveyed, more women in the 25-34 age group use contraceptives than in the younger group. The areas of Buenavista and Yateras show, together with Costa Rica, the highest values for contraceptive use in this age group. This must therefore have been an important factor in the marked decline in fertility in women over 30 years old in those areas.

Table 64. Percentage of women from selected developing countries who currently use contraceptives, according to age, number of living children, and type of residence, 1974-78 and 1982

Regions and countries	Present age (years)			Number of children alive				Type of residence		All women
	15-24	24-34	35-44	Less than three	Three	Four	Five and more	Urban	Rural	
Asia and the Pacific[a] (1974-78)										
Bangladesh	6.7	11.5	14.3	5.7	11.1	11.5	14.9	22.6	8.5	9.6
Fiji	43.3	57.6	62.9	36.8	56.3	66.5	73.1	61.7	53.1	56.2
Indonesia	22.2	41.5	42.4	26.3	46.6	42.9	50.7	22.4	27.9	36.8
Korea, Republic of	18.7	43.5	57.0	32.2	53.8	56.7	49.6	48.8	42.2	45.7
Malaysia	34.7	46.4	39.5	32.2	42.6	43.9	39.4	54.9	34.8	38.0
Nepal	0.9	3.7	4.9	0.9	2.9	4.7	9.1	-	2.9	2.9
Pakistan[b]	2.0	7.0	10.0	1.0	7.0	8.0	10.0	15.0	3.0	6.0
Philippines	36.5	50.3	51.1	38.6	54.8	54.1	49.7	59.7	41.6	47.7
Sri Lanka	24.4	43.0	48.3	28.1	48.0	52.6	50.7	48.9	39.5	41.4
Thailand[b]	35.2	49.9	48.5	38.1	53.0	58.5	46.7	48.7	35.1	45.6
Latin America[a] (1974-78)										
Colombia	48.7	60.1	49.3	57.5	56.3	58.3	48.2	62.0	34.0	52.0
Costa Rica[c]	77.1	80.5	78.8	74.9	83.4	80.2	70.0	81.1	74.5	77.8
Dominican Republic	32.9	50.9	43.5	32.2	51.4	49.9	45.1	48.9	28.8	41.7
Guyana	29.3	43.5	41.8	28.8	39.5	38.8	47.8	40.8	36.7	38.1
Jamaica[d]	42.8	52.5	43.7	39.2	45.1	51.9	53.4	50.8	40.2	44.5
Mexico[d]	31.7	47.3	43.5	38.8	46.7	46.2	40.4	60.7	22.5	58.5
Panama	55.9	68.1	65.9	64.2	71.1	69.7	62.3	72.4	55.7	65.1
Peru	34.9	47.5	40.8	41.0	48.1	43.2	37.5	44.6	14.7	41.3
Cuba[e] (1982)										
Plaza de la Revolución	24.3	67.0	58.3	62.2	69.3	60.5	52.0	67.1	-	67.1
Buenavista	29.4	73.3	73.9	71.5	78.7	80.4	80.3	73.7		73.7
Yateras	42.9	72.2	76.0	72.2	79.8	74.6	70.8	-	69.8	69.8

a Includes married and consensually married women, who live with their spouses, are considered fit to have more children, and were not pregnant at the time of interview.

b The percentage by place of residence refers to married women who are not pregnant.

c Refers to women from 20 to 44 years.

d Places with 20,000 inhabitants or more were considered to be urban localities.

e Includes single and ever-married women in general, without taking into account the considerations mentioned in a except for the urban-rural and "All women" columns where ever-married women were used.

Sources: Concepción, 1982; EDEMU-82.

The value for Plaza de la Revolución is also among the highest, with higher values registered only by two countries, Costa Rica and Panama, both of which have experienced reductions in fertility.

The proportions of contraceptive users according to the number of children were equally high, in all three areas. Once again, it should be remembered that in the case of Cuba the data refer only to areas and not to the country as a whole, but as there is an urban area, a semi-urban area and rural area, the comparison should not be considered too unrealistic.

Comparisons of proportions of contraceptive users according to urban or rural residence may perhaps be considered more acceptable as these values, unlike those according to age group and number of children, were estimated for married women and women in a consensual union only. It should be borne in mind, however, that Plaza de la Revolución is a wholly urban zone and Yateras is one of Cuba's most rural zones. Unlike the 18 WFS countries, in which the percentage of contraceptive users is higher in urban than in rural zones, the value for Yateras is slightly higher than that for the urban zone, Plaza de la Revolución. Here it should be stressed again that Plaza de la Revolución makes greater use of abortion as a method of regulating fertility than does Yateras.

The data presented in table 65 do not seem to reflect any remarkable differences in the use of contraceptives between women with different educational levels within the same area.

Table 65. <u>Percentage of women who have used contraceptives during the last month according to educational level</u>

Educational level	Plaza de la Revolución	Buenavista	Yateras
Primary	43.8	65.8	63.9
Basic medium	39.0	44.8	50.7
Higher medium	45.0	44.7	53.4
University	66.6	52.9	a

a Information not representative.

Source: EDEMU-82.

It would seem, for example, that in Plaza de la Revolución it is the women with a higher educational level who use contraceptives the most, while in Buenavista and Yateras it is the group with a "primary" level. Of course, these figures may be influenced by the age structure and the educational structure itself. It must be borne in mind that in Plaza de la Revolución's sample there are a good many women at the higher level while in Yateras the majority are at the primary level. The fact that knowledge of contraceptive methods and the facilities to obtain them are widespread throughout the country would in any case explain a more or less similar behaviour for any educational level.

Table 66 gives figures for the use of contraception on the part of women during the preceding month according to the educational level of their husbands. Women who are married or have a stable union are therefore referred to here. The main observation which can be made on table 66 is that in each area the use of contraceptives by married women and women in a consensual union is high in all educational categories. The average for Plaza de la Revolución is about 66 per cent, for Buenavista over 70 per cent and for Yateras about the same. There is, however, a slight tendency for contraceptive use to be greater among women whose husbands are more highly educated.

Table 66. <u>Proportion of women who used some form of contraception during the preceding month according to spouse's educational level</u>

Spouse's educational level	Plaza de la Revolución	Buenavista	Yateras
Primary	62.5	72.5	66.1
Basic medium	60.1	74.3	73.4
Higher medium	66.1	73.5	68.6
University	75.1	81.3	71.0

Source: EDEMU-82.

Women who had not used contraceptives were asked why. This information correlated with their own educational level, on the one hand, and with that of their spouse, on the other. Among those currently at risk of becoming pregnant, the majority answered either "I don't like it (or my husband does not)" or "I don't become pregnant". These two answers together totalled a little over 70 per cent in Plaza de la Revolución, about the same in Buenavista and around 60 per cent in Yateras. The explanation "Because I want to have all the children that come", on the other hand, was more frequent in Yateras than in the other areas, though not more than 11 per cent of women gave this answer (EDEMU-82, tables 193 and 196).

100

Table 67 analyses the information on women's use of contraceptives according to their labour situation and occupational group, distinguishing those women who have ever used them and those who currently use them.

What is immediately obvious is that there are considerable differences in contraceptive use between working and non-working women — although a high proportion of non-working women do in fact use them. What is also noticeable is the level of current

Table 67. Percentage of women who have ever used contraceptives and who currently use them, according to labour situation and occupational group

Area and labour situation	Ever used	Currently use
Plaza de de Revolución		
Not working	44.3	33.0
Working	80.2	53.4
Group I	81.1	56.3
Group II	77.4	49.5
Group III	85.0	51.6
Buenavista		
Not working	58.3	46.7
Working	79.7	64.6
Group I	76.4	61.4
Group II	84.8	66.5
Group III	75.7	69.8
Yateras		
Not working	70.9	56.5
Working	78.7	61.4
Group I	68.2	50.6
Group II	82.3	63.3
Group III	79.6	65.0

Source: EDEMU-82.

contraceptive use among the different occupational groups in Buenavista and Yateras which is higher among women in the occupational groups with lower qualifications. This trend is similar to the one found in the average number of abortions per woman.

There is also a clear relationship between the use of contraceptives and variations in the standard of living of interviewees. As shown in table 68, women with a higher standard of living are more likely to have resorted to contraception to control their fertility at some period, in all three areas. The values for women with a high standard are 24, 20 and 9 per cent higher than for those with a low standard, in Plaza de la Revolución, Buenavista and Yateras, respectively. Thus the effect of standard of living is most marked in Plaza de la Revolución and least in Yateras.

Table 68. <u>Percentage of women who have ever used contraceptives according to standard of living</u>

Standard of living	Plaza de la Revolución	Buenavista	Yateras
Low	58.5	64.7	76.6
Medium	62.5	68.2	74.5
High	72.0	77.5	83.3

Source: EDEMU-82.

CHAPTER VIII

SUMMARY

Fertility in Cuba has dropped rapidly since 1965 to levels typical of developed industrialised countries. The present monograph documents the nature of the fertility changes which have been occurring and investigates linkages to changes in women's roles and their improved status since the Revolution in 1959.

The analysis is based primarily on the results of a survey conducted in three very different locations with differing economic contexts and different fertility rates: the completely urbanised municipality of the capital city, Plaza de la Revolución, in the province of City of Havana; the totally rural municipality of Yateras, in the province of Guantánamo; and the semi-urban district of Buenavista, in the municipality of Cienfuegos in the province of the same name. In total, 3,302 women between the ages of 15 and 59 were interviewed.

The analysis proceeded on two main levels: first the socio-economic context resulting from the transformation of the Revolution and measures taken to promote sexual equality as well as to reduce rural/urban differences; and secondly, the changes which have been occurring in the direct determinants of fertility, in particular nuptiality patterns and the use of contraception and abortion. It is hypothesised that a key link between these two levels is the changes which have been occurring in the roles of women both inside and outside the family, which have affected women's ideals concerning conjugal relations, family size and spacing of births.

8.1 Socio-economic and demographic differences among the areas studied

Public services and public administration are the main activities in Plaza de la Revolución; the seat of government and most of the country's educational and cultural centres are located here. According to the 1981 census, the activity rate for women 15 years and over is 49.3 per cent. Yateras, by contrast, has important forest reserves, coffee production is the basic economic activity, and women's activity rate is 28.7 per cent. The area of Cienfuegos has an intermediate activity rate: 38.8 per cent. Economic activity here is mainly industrial in nature, with a port and some agricultural production on the outskirts. These contrast with activity rates of about 70 per cent for adult men in all three areas.

The average number of years of study for the population of the three provinces (also according to the 1981 census) is highest for City of Havana (8.3 years), followed by Cienfuegos (6.6) and Guantánamo (5.5). Educational differences between provinces, however, have diminished in a remarkable way between 1953 and 1981: the number of years of schooling has increased by 2.6 times in Guantánamo, 2.1 times in Cienfuegos and 1.7 times in City of Havana. Also, as far as health provision is concerned, the three provinces studied have fairly similar facilities, and low infant mortality rates, ranging from 15.9 per thousand in City of Havana to 21.6 in Guantánamo.

Looking at the standard of living in the three areas studied, it was found that housing conditions were considerably better in the more urban areas. Ninety-five per cent of houses were built of good-quality materials in City of Havana, 70 per cent in Cienfuegos and 58 per cent in Guantánamo.

According to preliminary estimates from vital statistics, Plaza de la Revolución registered a gross reproduction rate of 0.59 in 1981, while the rate for Cienfuegos was 0.80. Yateras registered the highest value of the three, and of the whole country: 1.40. The sex and age structure of the population also differs considerably according to degree of urbanisation, with a much older population structure and higher proportion of women to men in the more urban areas. The former is due mainly to differential fertility rates while the latter may well be linked to the very different patterns of internal migration prevalent in urban and rural areas: while City of Havana has a positive annual migration rate of over 4 per cent, Guantánamo has a negative rate of -7.4 per cent.

8.2 Characteristics of women in the areas studied

The survey results confirm that in all three areas a massive advance in women's education has taken place. There are still differences between areas but these are smaller in the younger age groups. The average number of years of study by women, according to the survey, is 9.6 years in Plaza de la Revolución, 7.4 in Buenavista, and 6.1 in Yateras. There is a significant difference here between the older and the younger women, however, particularly in Yateras, where the average number of years of schooling increased from three to seven years in one generation.

Women's participation in economic activity was found to be somewhat higher than in the 1981 census: 59.7 per cent of the women in the survey interviewed in Plaza de la Revolución were working for money, while for Buenavista the figure was 45.5 per cent and for Yateras 40.7 per cent (this latter figure was undoubtedly influenced by the timing of the survey, which was done during harvesting of the coffee crop). Among the economically inactive women, the proportion who are housewives increases as one goes from the urban to the rural zone, and among older age groups, while the proportion of students is highest in the youngest age group and in the more urbanised areas.

The urban zone has the largest proportion of married women among the interviewees, but Yateras has the most women in a consensual union; if we add together married women and women in a consensual union, it is Yateras which shows the highest value (73 per cent), followed by Buenavista (69 per cent) and Plaza de la Revolución (54 per cent).

With regard to marital problems, those most frequently mentioned in Plaza de la Revolución and Buenavista were those connected with the lack of participation by the husband in the care of children and in the housework, which together amounted to almost 72 per cent of the problems. In Yateras the most general problem was infidelity, but in Plaza de la Revolución and Buenavista this took third place.

8.3 Fertility in the survey areas and women's socio-economic characteristics

Fertility levels have declined considerably in the last ten years, particularly in Yateras, which had a very high level ten years ago. This has helped reduce the difference in fertility between the rural and urban areas, a fact also confirmed by studies made at the national level.

Fertility has become increasingly concentrated in younger age groups - that is, the proportion of total fertility accruing to women under 30 years old has increased markedly. The relatively high fertility of women from 15 to 19 years of age should be stressed. It is now a matter of priority for the Cuban State to encourage women to delay childbearing. This fertility pattern is very different from that shown by industrialised countries with low levels of fertility.

Although all three sample areas have low reproductive levels, there is still a tendency for fertility to be lower in urban areas than in rural areas, and among better educated women than less well educated women. The fact that educational levels are still improving throughout the country and that more rural areas will undoubtedly become more urbanised may produce further reductions in fertility levels - but possibly not very large reductions because of the already low levels.

Women's labour situation also has an influence on fertility levels: women working for money had lower fertility levels than non-working women. An increase in the labour force participation of women, such as has taken place in the last ten years, therefore has a significant effect in reducing fertility. Although there was a difference in fertility between women who were working and those who were not working at the time of the survey, with the general decline in fertility this differential has decreased in all three areas, although it is still greater in the most rural area as compared with the most urban.

Among working women there are noticeable differences in fertility levels according to occupational group, with lower fertility levels in the highest occupational categories. These differences increase as one moves from the most urban area to the most rural.

Standard of living also seems to have an influence on fertility, with noticeably lower fertility levels amongst women with a higher standard of living in all three areas. Variations in fertility between areas are greatest amongst older women with a low standard of living.

8.4 Ideal family size and birth spacing

With regard to the ideal number of children, less than 1 per cent of women felt it was ideal to have no children. In Yateras, however, almost 20 per cent did not have any chidren, and in Plaza de la Revolución 36.8 per cent. Although around 20 per cent of women in the three areas had one child, only 2 per cent of women in Plaza de la Revolución regarded this as ideal, and only 1 per cent in Buenavista and Yateras. In general, the ideal number of children was higher than the number of children women actually had and also higher than the number which current fertility rates would predict they would have. In all cases, however, the ideals were fairly low, around two or three children per woman. The number of children women wish to have seems to be affected more by where they live than by their educational level. Nor do family size ideals appear to be significantly affected by women's labour situation (working or not working) or occupational group.

With regard to ideal and actual intervals between marriage and the first birth and between births, there are some obvious differences between the three areas. Both ideal and actual intervals tend to decline as one moves from urban to rural areas. In no case does the average actual interval between marriage and first birth reach two years, even when the ideal is higher, as in Plaza de la Revolución and for most women in Buenavista. A relatively high proportion of women have their first child before the end of the first year of marriage, in all three areas, particularly the youngest women.

Women's educational levels do not seem to have any effect on the actual interval between marriage and the first birth,

106

though in Plaza de la Revolución and Buenavista women at higher educational levels tend to favour a slightly longer interval. The same is true of standard of living, though in Plaza de la Revolución this interval is noticeably shorter for women with a low standard of living. Women's labour situation and occupational group seem to have a negligible effect on both ideal and actual intervals.

There is in general a responsible attitude about when it is best to have a child, mainly related to the need for a greater degree of understanding between the couple. Amongst women with higher educational levels this attitude is marked in all three study areas. Having a child does not seem to be regarded by the interviewees as incompatible with being able to work or study.

Actual intervals between births do not accord with the ideals. While ideals become longer as one moves from the urban to the rural areas, the actual intervals become shorter. In Yateras women reported the shortest actual interval, most having their second child before the eldest was 2, while between 55 and 62 per cent of women in Plaza de la Revolución and Buenavista waited at least two years.

There is also a tendency for women with higher educational levels to have longer intervals between births, in all three areas. The actual interval also tends to be longer for women with a higher standard of living, except in Yateras.

Whether women do or do not work does not seem to affect spacing significantly, but there is a tendency for women in higher occupational groups to have slightly longer gaps between their children.

8.5 Ideal and actual age at first marriage

Ever-married women in all three study areas had married at earlier ages than they felt was the ideal age to marry.

Women's ideal and actual age at marriage depends more on where they live than on their educational level, being earlier in Yateras and Buenavista than in Plaza de la Revolución. However, actual age at marriage shows much greater variation between regions than does ideal age at marriage.

Irrespective of standard of living and area of residence, at least one out of two women said that the ideal age for a first conjugal union should be between 20 and 24 years. However, as the level of urbanisation decreases, there is an increased preference for an earlier age at marriage, 15-19 years old.

The different reasons women give to justify their ideal age

at marriage suggest that in the rural area it is believed that women "mature" or "finish their studies" a little earlier than in the urban area.

The first stable conjugal union usually occurs at a young age in all three areas, but especially in the semi-urban and rural areas. Working women tend to have married later than those who do not work, particularly in the urban and semi-urban areas. The analysis by occupational group also shows a trend towards later marriage in the occupations which call for higher qualifications.

Early marriage is one of the causes of the rejuvenation of fertility. The experience of other countries would lead one to expect that this early age at marriage would lead to higher fertility levels than those actually found in the three areas. This means that other factors exert an opposite influence and decrease the fertility of these women.

8.6 Conjugal situation

The fertility differentials between the three areas can clearly be related to the higher proportion of women under 30 years who are single in the more urbanised areas (20 per cent in Yateras compared to 57 per cent in Plaza de la Revolución).

A high proportion of women in consensual unions may also be related to a higher fertility level; in Yateras there were 307 women under 30 years old in consensual unions for every 100 married women, while in Plaza de la Revolución there were only 27 for every 100.

It was found that women in the highest occupational category were noticeably less likely to be in a conjugal union than women in lower occupational categories, in all three areas. This helps explain the low fertility of working women in Plaza de la Revolución, where a high proportion of working women belong to the higher occupational groups.

More than 25 per cent of the women interviewed had had two or more conjugal unions. Amongst women with higher educational levels, the proportion with only one union increases. This seems to indicate that their selection is more considered and more mature.

The proportion of working women who have had more than one conjugal union is higher than that for non-working women, both in the most urban area and in the most rural area. This suggests an association between women's labour activity and marital instability.

Apart from any association that may exist between women's

108

labour activity and the number of conjugal unions, there is another phenomenon involved here which has certainly been partially responsible for the high divorce rates the country has experienced during the last decade. At the centre of this process is the redefinition, at both the social and the family level, of the role of women within the framework of the new Cuban society, involving a much greater degree of participation by women in all spheres: economic, political, educational and cultural.

8.7   Abortion

Although the incidence of abortion has declined, it has played and still does play an important role in the regulation of fertility, particularly in the urban areas. The incidence of abortion is generally higher in the more developed area of Plaza de la Revolución, where facilities are more readily available. The average number of abortions per woman declined throughout the 1970s in both rural and urban areas, but particularly in the urban area where the incidence was greatest.

However, its incidence does not seem to be related to women's educational levels. The reason for this is the wide availability of health services and the high level of information people have, irrespective of educational level.

In both Plaza de la Revolución and Buenavista working women are more likely to have had abortions than non-working women. There is also a clear tendency for the incidence of abortion to be greater amongst women in the lower occupational categories.

8.8   Contraception

The level of knowledge of contraceptive methods is high - almost 100 per cent of sample women had some knowledge of contraception in all three areas, the intra-uterine device and the pill being the most widely known.

Contraceptive use is also consistently high in all three areas, with about 85 per cent of ever-married women having used a method and about 70 per cent currently using one. The contraceptive methods most used are highly effective ones: the intra-uterine device, followed by female sterilisation and the pill. The youngest women make least use of contraceptives, which partly explains their relatively high fertility.

Women's educational level does not seem to make an appreciable difference to the level of contraceptive use, but there are clear correlations between contraceptive use and women's labour situation. In all three areas, working women are more likely to use contraceptives than non-working women. This is especially marked in Plaza de la Revolución, where 80.2 per cent of working women had used contraceptives at some time, as opposed to 44.3 per cent of non-working women. The corresponding figures for Yateras are 78.7 and 70.9 per cent.

In conclusion, the continuing differences in fertility among the three regions studied do not seem to be attributable to differences in contraceptive use - at least currently. Greater frequency of abortion in Plaza de la Revolución is no doubt a factor lowering fertility in this urban area. Another factor would appear to be the higher proportion of women in Plaza de la Revolución who are not in a union (i.e. separated women and single women under the age of 30 years).

More generally, the overall fertility decline in Cuba must be understood in the context of the socio-economic development which has occurred: the rapid rise in women's educational levels, the spread of health facilities to the rural areas and the increasing participation of women both in the labour force and in community affairs.

APPENDICES
==========

Appendix 1

SAMPLING METHOD

The sampling method used was that of a single stage cluster sample with probability proportional to size. In Plaza de la Revolución and Buenavista the clusters were those defined in the 1981 Census, while in Yateras the clusters were areas grouped around a collection of houses.

Now let us look at the mathematical model which describes the sampling method.

Let us call Pi the probability of choosing the i-th cluster (i=1,2,...N), where N is the number of clusters in the population.

Since

$$\sum_{i=1}^{N} Pi = 1.$$

We will now introduce the following variable:

$$Zi_J = \frac{Mi\ Yij}{Mo\ Pi}. \qquad (1)$$

Obviously Mi will be the number of women in the i-th cluster and Mo the number of women in the population. It then follows that

$$Mo = \sum_{i=1}^{N} Mi.$$

It is easy to see that $Mi = \sum_{J} M_{ij}$, as M_{ij} will be defined as the number of women in the j-th nucleus of the i-th cluster.

On the other hand, Yijk is the value of the characteristic of the k-th woman in the j-th nucleus of the i-th cluster.

Hence, it can be affirmed that

$$\overline{Y}ij = \frac{1}{mij} \sum_{k}^{mij} Yijk,$$

where mij is the number of women in the j-th nucleus of the i-th cluster.

112

From (1) it is easy to see that

$$\bar{Z}i = \frac{Mi\ \bar{Y}i}{Mo\ Pi}\ ; \quad \text{where}\quad \bar{Y}i = \frac{1}{Mi}\sum_{J=1}^{Ni}\bar{Y}ij^{m}ij\ .$$

and Ni is the number of nuclei in the i-th cluster.

It is not difficult to demonstrate that the expected value of $\bar{Z}i$ is equal to the mean of the Y population, that is

$$E\ (\bar{Z}i) = \sum_{i=1}^{N} Pi\ \bar{Z}i$$

$$= \sum_{i=1}^{N} Pi\ \frac{Mi\ \bar{Y}i}{Mo\ Pi} \tag{2}$$

$$= \frac{1}{Mo}\sum_{i=1}^{N} Mi\ \bar{Y}i\ .$$

It is also known that (2) is the mean of the population, therefore

$$E\ (\bar{Z}i) = \bar{Y}$$

and with this it is proven that $\bar{Z}i$ is an estimator of Y.

As in our case the probability of choosing was proportional to the size of the cluster, in other words, $Pi = Mi/Mo$, then the Z variable has been identical to Y and $\bar{Z}_n = \bar{Y}_n$, that is

$$\bar{Z}_n = \frac{1}{n}\sum_{i=1}^{n}\bar{Z}i = \bar{Y} = \frac{1}{n}\sum_{i=1}^{n}\bar{Y}i$$

and this is the estimator used to estimate the mean of the population, which is also

$$E\ (\bar{Z}n) = E\ (\frac{1}{n}\sum_{i}^{n}\bar{Z}i) = \frac{1}{n}\sum_{i=1}^{n}E(\bar{Z}i) = \frac{1}{n}\sum_{i=1}^{n}\bar{Y} = \bar{Y}.$$

It is not difficult to show that the variance of Zn is given by

$$\sigma^2\ (\bar{Z}n) = \frac{\sigma^2 bz}{n}$$

where σ^2 refers to the variance of the mean by conglomerate, defined by

$$\sigma^2 bz = \sum_{i=1}^{n} Pi \, (\bar{Z}i - E\,(\bar{Z}i))^2.$$

On the other hand, the estimator of $\sigma^2\,(Zn)$ is given by

$$\hat{\sigma}^2\,(Zn) = \frac{s^2\,nz}{n}$$

where s^2_{bz} is the mean square between the conglomerates $\bar{Z}i$ in the sample, defined by

$$s^2_{bz} = \frac{1}{n-1} \sum_{i}^{n} (\bar{Z}i - \bar{Z}n)^2.$$

As Pi=Mi/Mo it follows that $\bar{Z}n = \bar{Y}n$, $\sigma^2\,(\bar{Z}n) = \dfrac{\sigma^2_b}{n}$ where

$$\sigma^2_b = \sum_{i\,1}^{n} \frac{Mi}{Mo}\,(\bar{Y}i - \bar{Y})^2 \qquad \text{and} \qquad \hat{\sigma}^2\,(\bar{Z}n) = \frac{s^2_b}{n}$$

eing

$$s^2_b = \frac{1}{n-1} \sum_{i=1}^{n} (\bar{Y}i - \bar{Y}n)^2.$$

114

SEX STRUCTURE, AGE STRUCTURE AND MASCULINITY INDEX OF THE POPULATION OF EACH MUNICIPALITY STUDIED, 1981

Age group	Plaza de la Revolución			Cienfuegos			Yateras		
	Males (%)	Females (%)	Masculinity index[a]	Males (%)	Females (%)	Masculinity index[a]	Males (%)	Females (%)	Masculinity index
0- 4	2.4	2.2	107	3.6	3.3	106	6.4	5.6	115
5- 9	3.7	3.5	107	5.0	4.8	105	7.8	7.4	105
10-14	4.6	4.5	102	6.1	5.7	106	8.5	7.7	111
15-19	6.1	6.0	101	6.0	5.7	104	6.6	6.1	108
20-24	3.4	3.7	96	3.8	3.9	96	4.8	4.3	112
25-29	2.9	3.3	87	3.4	3.5	97	3.5	3.3	105
30-34	3.1	3.8	84	3.6	3.7	96	2.6	2.5	104
35-39	3.4	4.2	81	3.3	3.5	94	2.3	2.2	102
40-44	3.6	4.1	87	2.8	2.9	97	2.1	1.8	119
45-49	2.7	3.4	80	2.2	2.4	93	1.9	1.5	127
50-54	2.5	3.1	80	2.1	2.1	95	1.6	1.3	131
55-59	2.1	2.7	76	1.8	2.0	90	1.4	0.9	156
60-64	1.8	2.6	68	1.6	1.8	91	1.2	0.6	182
65 and over	4.0	6.6	50	4.2	5.1	83	2.8	1.3	219
Total	46.3	53.7	86	49.5	50.5	98	53.5	46.5	115

a Refers to number of males for every 100 females.
Source: CEE, 1983, Vols. II, III and VIII, table 1.

Appendix 3

AGE STRUCTURE OF THE FEMALE POPULATION AGED 15 TO 59 YEARS IN EACH MUNICIPALITY AT THE TIME OF THE 1981 CENSUS

Age Group	Plaza de la Revolución		Buenavista		Yateras	
	EDEMU-1982 survey	1981 Census	EDEMU-1982 survey	1981 Census	EDEMU-1982 survey	1981 Census
15-19	18.0	17.6	21.5	19.2	24.3	25.7
20-24	12.0	10.5	14.6	13.2	20.5	18.1
25-29	8.8	9.6	12.3	11.7	15.0	14.0
30-34	9.2	10.9	11.9	12.5	10.9	10.6
35-39	11.8	12.3	10.5	11.7	9.4	9.1
40-44	12.3	12.0	8.4	9.8	6.1	7.4
45-49	10.5	10.0	9.3	8.0	5.2	6.1
50-54	9.0	9.1	7.8	7.2	4.6	5.2
55-59	8.4	8.0	3.8	6.7	4.0	3.8
Women from 15-59	100.0	100.0	100.0	100.0	100.0	100.0

Source: EDEMU-1982, table 1; CEE, 1983, Vols. II, III and VII, table 1.

Appendix 4

MEDIA CONTACT

An indicator was created in order to have a measure of the degree of contact that interviewees had with the media, thus completing our picture of the general educational and cultural level of the interviewees.

This indicator measures the frequency with which the women carry out activities which increase their knowledge of their surroundings: how often they read newspapers, magazines, and books, listen to the radio and watch television. Apart from frequency, additional value is given to reading as it is an activity which requires greater interest: while the other activities are carried out in the house, in this case the person has to go out of the house to borrow or buy the book.

According to the answers given, the interviewer can choose one of three alternatives:

Never: Interviewees who carry out this activity rarely or never. The value of this alternative is 0.

Sometimes: Those who carry out the activity regularly but not every day (around three times a week). The value of this alternative is 1 point.

Always: Interviewees who have made a habit of the activity, carrying it out every day or almost every day. The value of this alternative is 2 points.

The table where these answers are recorded is as follows:

How often ...

	Never (0)	Sometimes (1)	Always (2)	DK/DA (0)
... reads newspaper?				
... listens to radio?				
... watches television?				
... reads magazines?				
... reads books (2)?				

A total is obtained by adding all the figures in the table. Interviewees can then be classified into three categories:

Low contact   (0 - 3 points);
Medium contact   (4 - 8 points);
High contact   (9 -12 points).

Example 1

An interviewee answers that she:

... "usually does not read newspapers"	0
... "listens to the radio every day"	2
... "watches some television programmes"	1
... "very seldom reads magazines"	0
... "very seldom reads books"	0
Total	3

Example 2

... "reads newspapers sometimes"	1
... "listens to some radio programmes"	1
... "watches the three TV programmes she likes during the week"	1
... "only reads the two magazines she likes"	1
... "reads books sometimes"	2
Total	6

As can be seen, in example 1 the answers gain a total of 3 points; thus, according to the scale, this interviewee is considered to have a low level of media contact. In example 2, with a total of 6 points, the interviewee is held to have a medium level of contact.

Appendix 5

DESCRIPTION OF ACTIVITY CATEGORIES USED TO ANALYSÈ
THE LABOUR SITUATION OF INTERVIEWEES

Active

Was working: all women who were working for money, even if they were on vacation or leave.

Was looking for a job because she had lost it or left it: working women who had left or lost their jobs and were trying to find another one.

Was looking for a job for the first time: women who were making efforts to obtain their first paid job.

Inactive

Retired: women who received a pension because they had worked previously.

Student: women who regularly attended some educational centre that is part of the national education system.

Housewife: women who did not do any paid work, but devoted themselves to housework.

Other situation: women of working age who could not be placed in any of the previous categories.

Appendix 6

DESCRIPTION OF THE OCCUPATIONAL CATEGORIES
USED IN THE PRESENT SURVEY

Executives: Executives and leaders of state bodies and political and mass organisations; managers of national and local enterprises.

Professionals and technicians: Professionals and technicians involved at a high and medium level in all spheres of science, technology, education, research, medicine, culture and art.

Administrative workers: Office workers, including secretaries, typists, reproducing machine operators, receptionists, travel agency workers, filing clerks, administrative inspectors and others.

Service workers: Those working in the public food trade, dry cleaning, launderettes, hairdressing establishments and beauty parlours.

Agricultural workers (including forestry, hunting and fishing): Those involved in the rearing of cattle and poultry, and the handling of machinery, as well as other agricultural services and activities; those involved in the catching, cleaning, salting and processing of fish on board and similar activities in the different branches of the industry.

Non-agricultural workers: Those working in production in industry.

Others: Workers who cannot be classified by occupation.

Appendix 7

STANDARD OF LIVING INDICATOR

In order to obtain an approximate measure with regard to the status of the family, a standard of living indicator was created by grouping together three factors which together reflect the family's way of life:
(a) the possession of electrical household appliances;
(b) per capita income;
(c) average educational level of the members of the nuclear family aged 15 years and over.

All the information is obtained from the questionnaire regarding the nuclear family.

Method

(a) Possession of electrical household appliances

Electrical household appliances are categorised according to the possibilities of acquiring them, and are given the following points:

1 point	2 points	3 points	4 points
radio	electric fan	tape recorder	car
television	mixer	record player	air conditioning
refrigerator	washing machine		
	sewing maching		

If the family does not own any electrical household appliance, it gets no points. Each article owned will be given the corresponding points. The family will then be classified into one of four levels, according to the total number of points obtained:

```
1  - low          ( 1 -  4 points)
2  - medium       ( 5 - 12 points)
3  - high         (13 - 18 points)
4  - very high    (19 - 25 points)
```

(b) Monthly per capita income

This, too, is broken down into four categories:

```
1  -  very low    (less than $25)
2  -  low         ($25 - 55)
3  -  medium      ($56 - 95)
4  -  high        ($96 and more)
```

(c) Average educational level of members of the nuclear family aged 15 years and over

This is also broken down into four categories:

1 - low   (primary)
2 - basic medium   (basic   secondary,   qualified
                    workers)
3 - higher medium (medium technician, pre-university,
                    teaching)
4 - university   (university)

If a family member did not attain any of these levels, no points will be awarded.

To obtain the average level of the nuclear family, we took the educational level of each member according to the above classifications. If we add the points obtained by each person and divide the total by the number of family members, the result will correspond to the average educational level of the family. Decimal points between .1 and .5 are rounded down, while those between .6 and .9 are rounded up.

BIBLIOGRAPHY
============

Alvarez, L. 1982. La tendencia de la fecundidad en Cuba [Fertility trends in Cuba]. Havana, Ministerio de Salud Pública, Instituto de Desarrollo de la Salud.

---. n.d. Estudio de las mujeres en edad reproductiva, municipio de Yateras, Guantánamo, Oriente [Study of women of reproductive age in the municipality of Yateras, Guantanamo, Oriente]. Havana, Ministerio de Salud Pública.

---; Ruben, M. 1973. Encuesta de fecundidad en la región Plaza de la Revolución [Survey on fertility in the region of Plaza de la Revolución]. Havana, Ministerio de Salud Pública.

Anker, R. 1983. "Female labour force participation in developing countries: A critique of current definitions and data collection methods" in International Labour Review, Nov.-Dec., Vol. 122, No. 6.

Bodrova, V.; Anker, R. (eds.). 1985. Working women in socialist countries: The fertility connection. Geneva, ILO.

Bongaarts, J. 1982. The proximate determinants of natural marital fertility. Center for Policy Studies Working Paper No. 89. New York, Population Council.

Brass, W. 1974. Métodos para estimar la fecundidad y la mortalidad en poblaciones con datos limitados [Methods of estimating fertility and mortality in populations with limited data]. Series E, No. 14. Santiago de Chile, Centro Latinoamericana de Demografía (CELADE).

Centro de Estudios Demográficos (CEDEM). 1976. La población de Cuba [The population of Cuba]. Havana, Editorial de Ciencias Sociales.

Comité Estatal de Estadísticas (CEE). 1981. Boletín Definitivo de Inicio del Año Escolar 1980-1981 [Final Bulletin of the Beginning of the School Year 1980-1981]. Havana, Dirección de Educación, Ciencia y Cultura.

---. 1982. National Demographic Survey 1979. Havana, Dirección de Demografía.

---. 1983. Censo de Población y Viviendas de Cuba 1981. Ciudad de La Habana, Cienfuegos y Guantánamo [Census of the Population and Dwellings of Cuba 1981. City of Havana, Cienfuegos and Guantanamo]. Havana.

---. 1984. Anuario Demográfico 1983 [Demographic Yearbook 1983]. Havana, Instituto de Demografía y Censor.

---; CELADE. 1981. Cuba: El descenso de la fecundidad 1964-1978 [The decline of fertility in Cuba 1964-1978]. Havana, Dirección de Demografía and Santiago de Chile, CELADE.

Concepción, M. 1982. "Family formation and contraception in selected developing countries: Policy implications and WFS finding", in World Fertility Survey, 1981.

Davis, R.; Blake, J. 1967. "La estructura social y la fecundidad. Un sistema analítico" [Social structure and fertility. An analytical system], in Factores Sociológicos de la Fecundidad Humana [Social factors in human fertility]. CELADE and Colegio de Mexico.

Farnós, A.; González, F.; Hernández, R. 1985. "Cuba", in Bodrova and Anker, 1985.

Federation of Cuban Women. No date. Información sobre el comportamiento de la fuerza laboral femenina [Information on the behaviour of the female labour force]. Unpublished data.

Haub, C. 1981. 1981 World Population Data Sheet. Washington, DC, Population Reference Bureau.

Hernandez, R.; Rodriguez, O. 1982. "Problemas de la juventud en el mundo contemporaneo" [Problems of youth in the contemporary world], in Publicaciones CEDEM (Havana), No. 36.

ILO. 1984. Women, work and demographic issues: Report of an international seminar. Geneva.

Ministerio de Salud Pública (MINSAP). (n.d.) Informe Anual 1984 [Annual Report 1984]. Havana.

Miro, C. 1968. Un programa de encuestas comparativas de la fecundidad en América Latina: Refutación de algunos conceptos erroneos [A programme of comparative surveys of fertility in Latin America: Refutation of some mistaken concepts]. Series A, No. 49. Santiago de Chile, CELADE.

Mortara, G. 1948. "Determinação de fecundidade femenina segundo a idade conforme o Censo de 1940, a aplicações ao calculo da taxa de natalidade, de tábua de fecundidade e do coeficiente de reprodução, para a População do Brasil" [Determination of women's fertility by age according to the 1940 Census for the application of a calculation of the birth rate, of fertility tables and of the reproduction coefficient for the Brazilian population], in Revista Brasileña de Estadística (Rio de Janeiro), Año VIII, pp. 30-31.

World Bank. 1984. World Development Report 1984. Washington, DC.

World Fertility Survey. 1981. World Fertility Survey Conference 1980: Record of proceedings. Voorburg, Netherlands, International Statistical Institute.

World Health Organization. 1983. Statistics Annual 1983. Geneva.